Landscapes and documents

LANDSCAPES AND DOCUMENTS

Edited by Alan Rogers,
MA, Ph.D, FRHist.S, FSA
Senior Lecturer in Medieval and Local History, Department of Adult Education, University of Nottingham

and Trevor Rowley, BA, B.Litt, FSA
Staff Tutor in Archaeology, Department for External Studies, University of Oxford

Published for the Standing Conference for Local History by the Bedford Square Press of the National Council of Social Service, London

ISBN 0 7199 0883 3

Design and typography by NCSS Publications Department
at the Bedford Square Press of the National Council of Social Service
26 Bedford Square London WC1
Printed in England by Bowering Press Limited, Plymouth

Contents

List of Illustrations

Introduction

The papers contained in this book were first presented at a conference of adult education tutors at Bury St Edmunds in May 1972.

Since 1968 full-time adult education tutors in local history and archaeology have held separate annual meetings for the consideration of the subject matter and teaching methods related to their own disciplines. In 1972 it was proposed to hold a joint meeting to consider ways of bringing the two areas of study closer together. The main aim of the conference was to stress the necessity for all historians to use all types of evidence in their attempts to reconstruct the past. The archaeologist needs the documents, the documentary historian needs the fieldwork—and both need help from other disciplines, such as the geographer and the ecologist. Total history should be the aim of archaeologist and local historian alike.

Until recently, however, there has been very little real co-operation in practice. In part this has been due to a language problem. The archaeologist refers to two completely different aspects of his study when he uses the word 'archaeology'. He refers to the techniques of recovery and recording of the evidence, and at the same time he also implies the reconstruction of the past from that evidence. In the latter activity he comes nearest to the historian. The local historian however rarely distinguishes between two such activities. He is less conscious of the difference between his techniques of recovery and recording evidence and the process of reconstruction of the past in which he engages. It is this inability or unwillingness to separate functions which has helped to create the problems of dialogue between the archaeologist and the local historian.

There have of course been many other reasons for the lack of co-operation between them, besides a failure to appreciate that they are both basically engaged on the same task. Nevertheless, over the last twenty years local historical and archaeological studies have developed very rapidly. Both have flourished under the umbrella of adult education in university extra-mural departments. Inevitably, however, both of them have suffered growing pains, and there has been a tendency in both towards isolationism. Archaeology, in the south at least, has become preoccupied with the rescue situation, with the unprecedented destruction of its source material. There has been an obsession with retrieval of information. This has led in turn to an increasing emphasis on fieldwork in order to anticipate, if possible, the destruction of sites. This preoccupation can easily be justified by those involved in local archaeology although some of the more extreme postures adopted to gain public sympathy and money are open to, and often receive, criticism. On the other hand some archaeologists have responded to the rescue situation by ignoring it and becoming increasingly involved with the theoretical exercises of location analysis of what has become known as the 'new archaeology'.

Local history, on the other hand, has had a longer battle to fight to secure academic recognition—and the increasing amount of 'parish pump' (apart from 'mythological') local history has led to a feeling that local studies only really become significant when they are placed in a wider context or based on comparative studies. In many cases this too has led to an increasing emphasis on fieldwork, while the current upsurge of interest in 'conservation', especially of buildings, where the local historian is frequently called upon by the planners to supply information, has resulted in a great expansion of the techniques and application of relating documents to field surveys.

It was this sense of common interest, that both disciplines were becoming increasingly concerned with aspects of field studies, as well as a sense of guilt about their respective isolation, which brought the two groups of tutors together in 1972. The conference was originally planned to note some of those areas where co-operation was felt to have achieved some of the most significant results. Thus after an introductory paper by David Dymond, an opening up of the field by one who has worked on both sides of the fence, there were papers by Christopher Taylor on the whole range of his work for the Royal Commission for Historical Monuments in Dorset and Cambridgeshire, and by Peter Fowler on total archaeology and total history,* based on his experience of motorway surveys. Integrated studies by archaeologists were thus represented by Chris Taylor and Peter Fowler, and also by Tom Hassall of Oxford, who reported on early urban surveys, especially his own work at Oxford. This was followed by discussions of some of those ancillary disciplines which the historian is becoming more aware that he needs, the new geography* (by Chris Barringer of the Cambridge Board of Extra-Mural Studies) and ecological history by Dr Max Hooper. Then came two reports of significant work done, both on the local historian front. Rex Russell spoke of his work on parliamentary enclosures, and Barrie Trinder

---

* These papers are not included in the present volume.

(standing in at very short notice for Neil Cossons, Director of the Ironbridge Gorge Industrial Museum, and basing his paper on discussions with Mr Cossons) opened up the field of industrial archaeology.

This was the plan of the conference. But in fact the conference at an early stage (David Dymond's introductory paper) took a turn and concentrated on *one* method of achieving integration, the study of landscape history. Perhaps this was a result of the reluctance, which was still clearly felt by some present, to admit that there was a problem at all. There was some hesitation to accept that *all* aspects of historical study would benefit from a study of material remains, that no archaeologist could escape the need to look at documents. There were, for example, some suggestions as to the superiority of one type of evidence over the other. Indeed, it was still asserted that there were whole fields of study where documentary evidence could not apply at all, while in more recent periods the material evidence, although prolific, was relatively insignificant. We were, in fact, reluctant to come out of our corners, to abandon our chosen specialisms; and by thus choosing a neutral field, landscape history, where we could all agree that integrated studies were essential, the conference was able to discuss amicably the desirability of such an approach.

It is the view of the editors that we missed the point. Landscape studies are themselves only partial history, not total. Although it is highly desirable and satisfying to understand the landscape and its components, the landscape is essentially an 'archaeological' source. It is a much neglected source, and our fascination with it at the moment is understandable. Nevertheless, the landscape must take its place alongside other sources as part of the evidence surviving from the past. Archaeologists and local historians need to discipline themselves in the most effective use of landscape evidence, as of all other types of evidence. In our view Barrie Trinder's paper, in what follows, comes nearest to expressing the ultimate goal of the true historian.

Real problems however exist. There are as yet no satisfactory techniques for measuring and recording the evidence from the landscape—so that the archaeologist feels unhappy, for instance, with Christopher Taylor's suggestion below that field surveys can on occasion replace excavation, that adequate interpretations may be arrived at merely by walking and looking. There is also the problem of evaluating the comparative importance of apparently totally dissimilar forms of evidence, for example the post-holes of a medieval timber building compared with an inventory. There is always the danger, too, that each discipline will accept the conclusions of the other uncritically, conveniently forgetting the tendentious basis on which some of the arguments are based.

It is, of course, inevitable that archaeology and local history will ask different questions of landscape evidence; but it is our belief that, in rural as well as in the perhaps more obvious urban studies, the two should and eventually must work closely together.

One of the lessons to emerge from the conference was that co-operation should not be limited just to that period of history, from the seventh to the fifteenth centuries, which is common to medieval archaeologists and local historians. Both parties should think on a broader plane.

It was agreed at the conference that the papers should be published more or less as they were given. In order, however, to make the book more consistent with its revised theme, the papers of Peter Fowler and Chris Barringer have not been published here. Further, since Tom Hassall's paper is largely devoted to early urban surveys, and since there have been very significant strides made in later urban studies in the integration of the two subjects, the editors have invited Dr Vanessa Doe to add a paper on this topic. We sincerely hope that this has made for a more complete study of the theme of these essays, *Landscapes and documents*.

These papers are thus offered as a contribution to a continuing debate on the relationship between archaeological and historical studies, and especially towards an understanding of landscape history. Although they were prepared within the field of adult education, inevitably the debate has a wider significance. It is, we think, undeniable that most of the recent advances in this field have been made in a context of adult education, but the integrated approach to historical studies is spreading rapidly, in college, school and local societies, though perhaps most slowly of all in universities themselves.

The editors wish to express their thanks to the contributors for putting up so gallantly with the demands made upon them; to their publishers, the Bedford Square Press of the National Council of Social Service; to David Dymond and Peter Fowler for early discussions on the nature of this book; to Mrs Margaret Gosling for typing the manuscript.

ALAN ROGERS
TREVOR ROWLEY

Archaeologists and historians

David Dymond, *Tutor with the Board of Extra-Mural Studies, University of Cambridge, has worked as both an archaeologist and a local historian. He opens the discussion by examining the unsatisfactory relationship between the worlds of archaeology and history, and points to the development of landscape history as a means of improving the situation. His paper asserts that the student should more frequently be led by the nature of his interests to acquire proficiency in both fields, and that where material and documentary evidence exist side by side, the latter should be seen as having the greater potential—conclusions which many archaeologists and even some historians will find controversial.*

Rumour has it that there are industrial archaeologists who, in reply to an inquiry about the people who carried out a particular industrial process, will blandly retort 'What people?' Conversely, there are industrial or economic historians who will similarly ask 'What machines?' or 'What process?' Whether or not this is true, there is still a chasm between the worlds of history and archaeology, and our conference at Bury St Edmunds in May 1972 did nothing to show that it is noticeably closing. For half the time most of the local historians sat tight-lipped and faintly resentful as a succession of archaeological extroverts did their acts; by the time it was the turn of the local historians to describe their less spectacular work, most of the archaeologists had disappeared—no doubt back to frantic digging, money-raising and publicity-seeking (no disrespect is intended to either side!). Although extra-mural teachers might be expected to be particularly interested in inter-disciplinary developments, I must say that I saw little evidence of mutual interest and active dialogue.

Of course it is not easy to measure the present situation nationally, and we are all inclined to rely overmuch on impressions gained as researchers, readers, teachers, examiners, members of societies and so on. I presume that nearly all the points which were made at our conference about the desirability of relating historical and archaeological evidence were acceptable *in principle* to everyone present. It would be an insult to the work of many scholars to say, for example, that the study of churches and their fittings is not part of religious history, that the study of strip-lynchets and railways is not part of economic history, or that the excavation of towns, villages and cemeteries is not part of Anglo-Saxon history. The difficulties come of trying to put such principles into practice.

One deterrent is undoubtedly the vast amount of work to be done in purely documentary or archaeological research, without attempting any sort of overlap or correlation. By temperament and habit, most specialists understandably prefer to stay securely within the field in which they were initially trained. As Elton has expressed it, 'few men, thoroughly soaked in the waters of one historical pond, feel inclined to swim in another'.[1] On the one hand, the opportunities for documentary research grow constantly as ever more sources are found, deposited, catalogued and transcribed. On the other, in the vast perspectives of prehistory and protohistory, the archaeologist is steadily amassing knowledge by new discoveries, by the refinement of established principles and by methodological break-throughs such as carbon-14 dating or the recovery of buried seeds and pollens.

Even so, there is hardly an historical theme which does not have its topographical or archaeological dimension: the student of the Poor Law is unwise to ignore the physical character of the workhouse, and even the high-priests of history who study politics and government should not overlook administrative areas, boundaries, meeting-places and physical communications. Conversely it is indefensible for archaeologists to ignore documentary evidence which may have a bearing on their sites or areas: at their best such contacts will lead the archaeologist to far higher levels of interpretation than he can normally achieve. Human history is such a complicated blend of the intellectual and the physical, of mind, eye, body and place, that we ought not to carve it up arbitrarily in response to our own myopic vision. It is the past itself which should finally determine our reactions and methods, not simply our narrow academic training.

Then there are various technical difficulties which may deter people from correlating both kinds of evidence. For example, the archaeologist may not be prepared to learn palaeography and medieval Latin, and the historian may not be inclined to master the methods of field-reconnaissance and excavation. In my view these difficulties are often grossly exaggerated. If one is fascinated by a particular historical theme or problem, then one either acquires the techniques which are demanded by the evidence, or one co-operates with other specialists who can supply those techniques. Historical geographers are one group who manage to relate physical and documentary evidence without undue methodological difficulty; although their adoption of the techniques of archaeological fieldwork is slow, they make critical use of an increasingly large number of documents and relate them successfully to the physical world.[2] The main point is not that the technical difficulties are particularly daunting, but that too many people believe in them, or pretend to believe in them. As time goes on, more opportunities arise to learn these techniques and to practise them under real conditions: one thinks for example of training courses in archaeological excavation and fieldwork, and of specialist classes in palaeography run with the co-operation of county record offices.

Finally there are people who seem deterred by poorly-defined and prejudiced notions—often with more than a grain of truth—about the other discipline and its practitioners. For example some archaeologists tend to regard documentary research as essentially dull, rarefied and solitary; they may even distrust it because there is little in the way of a 'new history' (save perhaps the search for more reliable quantification in, for example, demography and economic history); they may deplore its seeming irrelevance to the present day, for there is no denying that archaeologists have far better contacts with the general public, and are more involved with contemporary life and its problems, than their historical colleagues. On the other hand, it is abundantly clear that many historians greatly distrust the frantic rumpus of contemporary archaeology, and claim to see minimal historical conclusions emerging from a cumbersome and time-consuming methodology. They point out that when interesting conclusions do emerge nowadays, they seem to come, more often than not, from palaeobotanists, zoologists, chemists and physicists rather than from archaeologists proper. They also ask how the archaeologist can concentrate on essential research programmes and on the necessity of refining techniques of recovery and interpretation if he is constantly being diverted by rescue operations. In spite of welcome trends towards total and large-scale excavation, and towards the ever more painstaking recovery of data, it would seem that we are recording a smaller proportion of what is actually being revealed and destroyed than was the case twenty years ago.[3] Archaeology, it appears, has never been so desperately short of time and money commensurate with its task.

These mutual criticisms are all justified up to a point, but they are invariably made from the comfort of the sidelines. The historian has to learn to accept that archaeology is by its very nature more popular, more urgent, more expensive, more gregarious, more cumbersome, and much closer to the natural and physical sciences. The archaeologist must accept that history is more securely established (therefore less experimental), more solitary, more inbred and self-sufficient, and, it must be said, more intellectually penetrating of the past.

Furthermore, there are fascinating differences of personality, which are emerging all the more strongly in the younger generation. The conference at Bury St Edmunds confirmed me in the view that practical history and archaeology appeal, quite often, to different kinds of people. The historian, devoted to the virtues of detachment and critical judgement, is a more withdrawn and circumspect creature than his archaeological opposite who, faced by complicated organisational problems, is increasingly likely to display some of the qualities of the property developer or TV personality! Or, as M. W. Thompson more guardedly puts it, 'the temperament that produces one seems often to exclude the other'.[4]

Whatever the reasons, the fact remains that the vast majority of teaching and researching historians and archaeologists do not bother to put the principles of co-ordination into use, and have little enthusiasm for them. The task is therefore undertaken by a tiny but growing minority who particularly wish to investigate some connection between man and his physical environment, whether as farmer, builder, traveller, manufacturer or whatever. For example, there are topographical historians or historical geographers, who in their study of settlement or field-patterns rely heavily on the interpretation of those highly specialised documents, maps; there are some students of vernacular architecture who are prepared to use inventories, surveys and deeds; a few industrial archaeologists assiduously search business archives. Conversely there are some medieval historians who are prepared to co-ordinate their documentary studies with art or architecture, as well as economic and agricultural historians who have related their documents to buildings, earthworks and even excavations. In these areas of history, problems are solved not, as we suggested at our conference, by mysteriously choosing the 'best' evidence available, but by using *all* available evidence which is *relevant* to the problem, whether documentary, archaeological, oral or scientific.

In the present situation, it seems to me that there are two matters for profound regret. The first is that far too many opportunities for convincing co-ordination are let slip by people who are easily deterred by the considerations mentioned above. Mainly because all kinds of physical evidence are fast disappearing (below *and* above ground),[5] this kind of co-operation should be developing much faster than it is. But secondly and beyond the needs of the moment, we are also missing parallel opportunities of a broader and more philosophical kind. Studies which employ both 'documents and landscapes' immediately make us aware of the inadequacy of our normal definitions, particularly in our uncritical use of key words like *history*, *archaeology*, *historical geography* and *documents*. For example, when most of us would define archaeology as the study of various unwritten physical remains, ought we to accept Colin Platt's bland suggestion that medieval archaeology combines the skills of historian and archaeologist?[6] Interdisciplinary studies also help us to focus attention on the variable nature of historical evidence, and the different methods of analysis and interpretation. In other words they emphasise history (in the broad sense) not as a body of knowledge, but as a set of critical techniques for reconstructing the past as fully and truthfully as possible. The person who really correlates physical and verbal evidence (and there are quite a few who pretend to, and do not[7]) will inevitably teach himself a great deal about the precise character of both kinds of evidence, their strengths and weaknesses, their relative value in given situations, and the problems of their so-called co-ordination.

Objects and words

I was reprimanded at the conference for divorcing history and archaeology and stressing their differences. For this I give no apology. Only by knowing the precise nature of both kinds of evidence (and they *are* different) and their respective techniques of recovery and interpretation, can one hope to co-ordinate them effectively. Historical evidence consists of verbal statements of great variety, which have a potential bearing on all aspects of human experience; archaeological evidence consists of man-made and natural objects (eg artifacts, monuments, strata, plant and animal remains, complete landscapes) which lead to firm conclusions mainly in the fields of technology and economics, and have recently enabled specialists, with the help of new scientific techniques, to reconstruct with greater accuracy the natural and man-made environments of the past. Not only are words and physical objects totally different in themselves, but they need quite different treatment if they are to be criticised and interpreted aright. How then is it possible to correlate them?

We have to show by reasoned argument that certain archaeological and historical 'facts' are concordant, or rather not discordant, and that they could therefore apply to the same events, conditions and places. We cannot for example prove that a particular medieval building *must* be the one referred to in an early document, but we can make out a case for their *probable* identification. A building has much greater interest and significance if relevant documents survive, and *vice versa*: the material remains are seen against the recorded actions or decisions of named people at specific dates, whereas the normally disembodied statements of a document gain physical expression when related to material remains. The two kinds of evidence are carefully arranged in an interpretative scheme which seems to make sense conceptually, chronologically and territorially.[8]

In a documented period, archaeology yields much information which documents could theoretically give, but often in practice do not. Therefore in trying to co-ordinate the two, we are attempting to create a fuller and better balanced interpretation of social and economic history. But it would be wrong to think of co-ordination as a process of simple *addition* in order to produce a longer piece of written history. Words and objects do not precisely slot into one another like pieces of a jigsaw, nor do they neatly overlap at specific points. The whole purpose of the exercise is to allow them to interact in our minds, so that they expose each other's fullest implications and deficiencies, and lead to a probabilistic interpretation which, being more complex, is nearer the goal of historical truth than a purely one-sided view.

It is important to note that where there seems to be a conflict between documents and material remains, the fault lies, not in the past itself, but in our interpretation of difficult or incomplete evidence. Sooner or later, it becomes apparent that one has not seen the full significance of one or both sides, and that by critical adjustment it is possible to make them concordant. It is not sufficient for the archaeologist to say, as he often does on these occasions, that archaeological evidence does not lie: it is the archaeologist himself who can lie or rather misinterpret, just as the documentary historian can.

Quantitatively the proportions of the two kinds of evidence constantly vary according to period and subject. For example the sparseness of documentary evidence in Pagan and Middle Anglo-Saxon times means that we are heavily reliant on archaeology. In the Middle Ages, documents like charters, surveys, rentals and court-rolls are relatively abundant, but the modern archaeologist is still able to revolutionise our knowledge of social and economic life, particularly where the peasant-farmer and ordinary town-dweller are concerned.

But qualitatively one soon recognises that written or verbal evidence goes much further than the merely physical: it touches a greater range of human activities, and brings one closer to the full capacity of the human mind. In a well documented period, it should be acknowledged without prejudice that archaeology is in a clearly subordinate position, and is, to paraphrase O. G. S. Crawford, 'a handmaid to documentary history'. Archaeology is the art of squeezing human thoughts and ideas out of fossilised actions and natural events. This is inevitably a more limited and less direct form of history than critically interpreting the actual statements of human beings in the past, which is what the documentary historian does. The historian actually starts with thoughts relating to most aspects of human life, whereas the archaeologist tries to create those limited human thoughts which are implicit in material remains.

All these considerations are excellently illustrated in an important recent book on deserted medieval villages.[9] Maurice Beresford, as a documentary historian, was able to discuss the rise and fall of population, wages and prices, changes in agriculture, the new attitudes of landlords, the break-up of the manorial system and the emergence of new social classes; in short, he is concerned with statements, ideas, personalities, decisions, absolute dates, and events of great variety. John Hurst, as an archaeologist, has had to work under 'more severe restraints', but has, nonetheless, distilled information of great historical value from fieldwork, excavation and typological study. For example, he reveals fascinating characteristics of medieval life, which many documentary historians and historical geographers had never even guessed: the very short life of medieval peasant-houses, their frequent re-alignment, widespread changes in building materials in the late twelfth and thirteenth centuries, and major changes in the plans of villages. But in common with all archaeological interpretation, Hurst's account is mainly an argued reconstruction of basic human activities such as building a house, digging a ditch or cobbling a yard. As soon as the attempt is made to explain *why* anything was done or happened (ie what human motives were involved), then considerable uncertainty can arise. Hence the frequency of phrases like 'the reasons for this change are hard to understand'.[10] Beresford's documents can reveal, potentially and actually, far more of the complexities of human motivation (and therefor history in the broadest sense) than can Hurst's buildings and pottery. In my view, therefore, one of the main advantages of medieval and post-medieval archaeology is that, while it stresses the undeniable importance of physical evidence in well-documented periods, it also highlights the essential limitations of that evidence as compared with the greater interpretative potential of the written word.

There has been a great deal of talk recently about writing history with the emphasis either on 'people' or 'place'. Alan Rogers has tried to dichotomise local history by saying that 'either the local historian is more concerned with the *place* that he is studying or with the *people* who formerly lived there'.[11] Similarly Alan Everitt has talked of two branches of local history, 'the study of the local community' and 'the development of the local landscape'.[12] To me both these statements are too simplistic because they confuse topics with evidence, and are not fair to those who attempt a real co-ordination of history and archaeology. The fact is that for generations topographical historians and archaeologists have been careful to state that they were not studying place or physical evidence for its own sake, but in order to understand human life in the past. Perhaps Mortimer Wheeler put this best in a memorable phrase written nearly twenty years ago: 'the archaeological excavator is not digging up things, he is digging up people'.[13] This is an important truth, but it still does not take us the whole way. Those of us who use 'documents and landscapes' are concerned more specifically with the ever-changing *relationship* between man and his physical environment, and see this as an historical theme every bit as important as political and constitutional affairs. Such an interest also has the important intellectual function of bridging the human and non-human sciences: for example, it encourages historians and archaeologists to converse and co-operate with ecologists, zoologists, botantists, soil-scientists and many others. It really is no dishonour to acknowledge an interest in the relationship between people and place, in spite of what Geoffrey Elton might say!

Continuity and change

Although it is fashionable nowadays to stress history as the study of change,[14] it seems more realistic to see it as constant tension between forces tending to produce change and forces tending to preserve the *status quo*; between, in other words, the two principles of change and continuity. In fact, the balancing of these is surely one of the main purposes of acquiring historical knowledge at any level: how far, we ask, have things changed and how far have they remained stable? Nowhere is the importance and subtle interplay of these two principles better illustrated than in landscape history.

On the one hand, we are concerned with measuring the continuity or stability of landscape features (and the human history which they represent). For example, just how old is a field-system or the plan of a village? How long has a particular site been continuously occupied? Can this patch of woodland be accepted as the natural descendant of prehistoric forest? These are questions which we are obliged to ask out of natural curiosity, and by excavation, fieldwork and documentary research, we hope that we can find some of the answers. The recent work of D. J. Bonney is an excellent example of what can be done. By careful surface fieldwork, coupled with the interpretation of Anglo-Saxon charters, tithe maps and other documents, he has made out a strong case for the continuity of some boundaries and estates in Wessex from pagan Saxon and even pre-Roman to modern times.[15] Sometimes however, the incompleteness of our evidence and its fundamental limitations mean that we are not so successful. For example, continuity of settlement is very difficult to establish, as it is often open to the objection that long or short periods of abandonment *may* have interrupted the history of a site.

So by the term continuity, we mean the extent to which features have not only been physically stable, but have also been used continuously for much the same purposes over considerable spans of time. If it is also possible to say when a feature was first created, however approximately or relatively, then so much the better. In practice, though, we are often restricted to giving a *minimum* age, that is, a date by which a particular feature was certainly in existence (and that may be a considerable underestimate of its true age). This kind of history, rooted in the imaginative interpretation of difficult or incomplete evidence, is very different from the uncritical and almost emotional desire displayed by some historians and historical geographers (particularly in the field of village-morphology) to push too far back in time.

On the other hand, much archaeological and topographical work measures the degree to which landscape features have changed over the centuries. In fact, physical evidence by its nature allows us to study change more readily than continuity, for the vital principle of stratification is basically a reflection of movement or process in time. Sometimes change in the landscape can be sudden, wholesale and dramatic, as when a settlement is abandoned (for example, a Roman villa in the fourth century or a complete village in the fifteenth) and a particular 'stream of life' is broken abruptly. The archaeology of abandonment may in some contexts be more difficult to recover and interpret, but historically it is just as important to know how occupation ends and what land-use succeeds it, as it is to know the archaeology of settlement.

However, change has many other more frequent and subtle manifestations. Paradoxically, a measure of change is always implied by continuity itself. A humble field-ditch dug 120 years ago as part of parliamentary enclosure will have been recut, cleaned and thereby modified many times; settlements continuously occupied for many centuries have often expanded and shrunk at different periods, in response to demographic and economic trends; vernacular buildings are constantly adapted to new standards of living and new social groups; churches have repeatedly been neglected, restored and refitted as they reflect changes in local population, wealth, religious enthusiasm and liturgical standards. Nobody can fail to be impressed by the complicated structural history of the church at Wharram Percy, as revealed recently by architectural historians and excavators.[16] Although this site has witnessed continuity of worship for at least a thousand years, from late Anglo-Saxon times until the twentieth century, the fabric of the church has undergone repeated modification and rebuilding, at first tending to grow in size and then to contract.

The current debates on the evolution of English villages and the continuity of Romano-British life into the Anglo-Saxon period, are making us think much more carefully about the different manifestations and interactions of continuity and change. The fact that a Romano-British farmstead or village was abandoned does not necessarily mean that the community (or part of it) did not survive on a nearby site, or that its farming activities completely ceased, or that its economic territory within certain boundaries was abandoned. Similarly it is clear that the early *community* implied in English or Scandinavian place-names and recorded in the pages of Domesday Book, need not necessarily have always lived on the same *site* as the present village. As more evidence accrues from excavation, surface fieldwork and documentary research, so our use of these two vital principles of continuity and change will become more penetrating and we shall be able to reconstruct more fully the complexities of man's relationship with his environment.

Notes

1 G. R. Elton, *The Practice of History* (1967) p. 71.
2 See for example Baker, Hamshere & Langton (eds), *Geographical Interpretations of Historical Sources* (1970).
3 For the resultant problems of recovering complete settlement patterns see C. C. Taylor, 'The study of settlement patterns in pre-Saxon Britain', in *Man, Settlement and Urbanism*, ed. Ucko, Tringham & Dimbleby (1972).
4 *Medieval Archaeology* XIII (1969) p. 299.
5 For an estimate of the pace of destruction, see Peter Fowler (ed.), *Archaeology and the Landscape* (1972) chap. IV and its two appendices.
6 Colin Platt, *Medieval Archaeology in England* (1969) p. 1.
7 Many of the guide-books to ancient monuments, published by the Department of the Environment, are a good example, with their separate unrelated sections on history and archaeology.
8 I have attempted to describe this process at greater length in *Archaeology and History* (Thames & Hudson, forthcoming).
9 Maurice Beresford and John Hurst (eds), *Deserted Medieval Villages* (1971).
10 Hence also the archaeologist's characteristic use of the passive tense (which is unavoidable) and of animistic language attributing human traits to material objects (which is avoidable, as Hurst shows).
11 Alan Rogers, *This was Their World* (1972) p. 4.
12 Alan Everitt, *Ways and Means in Local History* (1971) p. 5.
13 Sir Mortimer Wheeler, *Archaeology from the Earth* (1956, Pelican) p. 17.
14 For example, E. H. Carr, *What is History?* (1964, Pelican) p. 132; Alan R. H. Baker, 'Rethinking Historical Geography', in *Progress in Historical Geography*, ed. A. R. H. Baker (1972) esp. pp. 15–17.
15 Desmond Bonney, 'Early boundaries in Wessex', in *Archaeology and the Landscape*, ed. Fowler (1972).
16 See *Medieval Archaeology* XIII (1969) pp. 252–3; Deserted Medieval Village Research Group, Report No. 19 (1971) pp. 32–3.

Total archaeology or studies in the history of the landscape

In this paper Christopher Taylor, *a member of the staff of the Royal Commission for Historical Monuments and author of two recent studies of Dorset and Cambridgeshire, outlines the equipment and skills needed by the landscape historian. He raises the important issue as to whether these studies can best be done by one person (the polymath) or by co-operative enterprise (teamwork)—the former being the traditional approach of the local historian, the latter the method of the archaeologist.*

The study and teaching of local history and archaeology, as with many other disciplines, have inevitably tended to become more and more specialised in recent years. The local historian for example tends to analyse in great detail the effects of parliamentary enclosure in a few parishes, or wills and inventories, over a relatively short period of time. Everywhere there are local history groups and classes studying their individual parish with little thought to the wider significance of their work or its results.

The archaeologists, and here I mean archaeologists in the widest sense as those interested in all the material remains of the past, are even more specialised. There is now not only a Prehistoric Society and a Medieval Archaeological Society, but a Hill Fort Study Group, Medieval Moats Research Group, Historic Gardens Society and even a Brick Research Group. Very shortly it will become impossible for one archaeologist to understand what any other archaeologist is talking about. We are already very close to this. Long articles on Saxon metal work, recently published, can scarcely be fully understood by more than half a dozen people in the country, while the same applies to modern papers on medieval roofs, Bronze Age beakers or nineteenth-century military fortifications.

Of course we cannot deny that this specialisation is vital. By it the frontiers of our knowledge are pushed forwards and outwards, and therefore it must continue. However, many of us who both teach and carry out research in the related studies of local history and archaeology, and in particular try to correlate these studies into the history of the landscape, believe that other approaches to our disciplines are not only possible but also desirable. First and foremost, as teachers in the adult education world, I believe that it is our duty to widen the horizons of our students in their understanding of the past, not to narrow it down to the nearest excavation trench or the most easily understood glebe terrier, however interested we might be in them, or indeed however interesting we can make them seem to the students. In addition, in the increasingly detailed studies of Iron Age post holes, Roman pottery, seventeenth-century houses and nineteenth-century census returns, there is a serious danger that history, in its widest sense as the story of man, his achievements, his failures, his hopes and his disappointments, is either lost or totally forgotten. It is easy to forget that the crude Saxon pot that will not fit into our preconceived typological sequence may have been made by a woman who had quarrelled with her husband one morning; or that the ill-proportioned elevation of an eighteenth-century house could be the result of the incompetence of a local builder trying to follow the fashionable demands of an ill-educated member of the rising gentry; or that the obviously incomplete record of taxpayers in a small medieval village may be due to the fact that the collector was bribed to omit the majority of the inhabitants. More important, specialisation can result in the loss of the whole scope of history, with its great themes of the struggle of man against man and man against nature, and the achievements of man working with man and man working with nature.

This is not to say that there are no dangers in the non-specialised study of history. There are indeed and they have often been expressed. However, there is a place for an overall broad approach, especially in the world of adult education teaching and more particularly within the specific field of landscape studies. This broad outlook involves us in the entire history of the whole landscape in all its various forms from the earliest times to the present day. It has been called 'total archaeology' but 'landscape history' is perhaps more correct, for it involves the study of all aspects of the natural and man-made landscape and their correlation. It is not an easy field of study for either teachers or students to embark on. To do it successfully means being part geologist, geomorphologist, geographer, botanist, archaeologist, historian, archivist, architectural historian and much else. Certainly no one can be all these, but at least one ought to make the attempt. Indeed, one of the great advantages of working in the field of adult education is that sooner or later students with the appropriate background, interest or ability to tackle most of these disciplines appear in classes and all work together.

Three essential tools

The necessary accomplishments to achieve the proper study of total archaeology or landscape history are considerable. Without suggesting that the ideal tutor or students will ever turn up, there are I think certain basic attributes needed for the successful total archaeologist or landscape historian. First and foremost is an ability to appreciate landscape in all its forms. This is certainly the most difficult of all. Most of us, by training or inclination, see certain aspects of the landscape but not others. Each member of a group of specialists walking across a piece of country has a totally different view. The field geologist can, by observing changes in soil colour and texture, identify the division between the Upper and Lower Chalk, a feature that in some places provides a springline on which human settlement is based. The botanist will recognise plants such as dog's mercury and herb paris in the copses which indicate old and perhaps primary woodland left behind during medieval assarting (see Max Hooper's paper following). The geomorphologist can see a line of low rounded gravel knolls that are a small esker chain deposited under or just in front of an ice sheet. Here Roman engineers, medieval peasants and twentieth-century road construction gangs may have dug for road metal. The prehistorian picks up worked flint flakes that show him where earlier people lived, while the medieval field archaeologist notices minute traces of ridge and furrow which indicate where medieval farmers cultivated their fields. The vernacular architectural historian will recognise the layout of a late-medieval house even though it is entirely encased in nineteenth-century brick, and the architectural historian quickly sees that the involuted capitals on the columns of an eighteenth-century house indicate the work of a particular designer.

Individually all these are of interest, but when put together they are all part of the story of the whole landscape which is of even greater interest and of considerable educational value. Therefore the ability to *see* all these things, indeed to see everything, is the basis of total archaeology. Not, in the first instance, to *understand* all one sees; this is impossible. Just to notice that these features exist is enough to begin with. Later on experience and research will provide some of the answers as to how they all fit into the complete landscape and into social, economic and political history as well.

The great difficulty is that most people either do not see anything, or see only their own specialised interest and not what this might mean in wider terms. For example, relatively few people when walking through a town look above the shop fronts. If they do, they concentrate on the aesthetic effect (or otherwise) of the street elevations. But any town in this country tells us much of its history, whether it is the prosperity of merchants in the fifteenth and sixteenth century as at

Fig. 1 Horse-breeding paddocks near Newmarket, Suffolk. An unusual pattern on the English landscape, these fields are surrounded by artificial strips of dense woodland so as to provide shelter (and incidentally secure fencing) for the young animals; but the pattern of fields reflects earlier land use. The trees lining the road across the centre of the photograph reflect social pretensions; they are planted on the wide verges used for exercise runs.

By courtesy, B.K.S. Surveys Ltd

Exeter,[1] fashionable aims of the rich townsfolk in the eighteenth century as at Bath,[2] the pattern of earlier land holding and the pressures of industrialisation of the nineteenth century in say Leeds or London,[3] or the greed of developers or the inefficiency of local authorities in twentieth-century cities all over the country.

If people are interested in these things, are they also interested in fields? Not only can hedgerows now be dated by examining and counting their botanical content (see below, p. 42) but it is also possible to recognise fields in south Wiltshire cleared from the forest in the twelfth century,[4] fields enclosed from the downland or moorland in the seventeenth century in places as far apart as Dorset[5] and Yorkshire,[6] nineteenth-century parliamentary enclosure fields anywhere in midland England[7] and twentieth-century horse-breeding paddocks near Newmarket in Suffolk (Fig. 1).[8] These all differ in form, layout and, if hedged, botanical content. Although their exact date may require detailed research, if their physical appearance is not noticed most of their history in economic and social terms and all of their importance in the development of the landscape will be lost.

And who looks at railways? A number of devoted enthusiasts study them for their own intrinsic value, but what of their wider significance? The small and now abandoned Old Stamford station in Lincolnshire, built in a curious 'Jacobethan' style, is of considerable interest in the history of the nineteenth century. The station reflects the ancient and still continuing influence in the town of the Cecil family at nearby Burghley House which overlooks the town, and tells much of the social attitudes, aristocratic power and railway politics of the early steam age. Likewise the sharp bend just outside Dorchester station, Dorset, which still slows trains to this day, is the result of an extraordinarily early and successful attempt to preserve an archaeological site, and may be seen as one of the first victories for the environmentalists about whom so much is heard today.[9]

Again what of houses? We either just admire the fine Elizabethan manor house or pretty thatched seventeenth-century cottage or examine every brace and collar purlin. But the landscape historian must also look at houses of all dates as places where people lived. He must find out the type of people who built and constantly modified them and try to understand the pressures of population, tradition, fashion, convenience and economics which controlled or affected their building materials, construction, layout and appearance. It is not difficult to see how the traditional three-roomed house plan of countless seventeenth-century and early eighteenth-century small houses in the midlands and East Anglia probably evolved from the older medieval arrangement as a result of changing social and economic conditions. But first the fact that a standard house type actually exists must be ascertained by careful observation.[10] Similarly, the fact that many thousands of seventeenth-century and eighteenth-century rural houses were subdivided into two or three tenements in the early nineteenth century to cope with the rural population explosion, recorded in the official census returns, is of great importance in terms of rural society. The physical manifestation of this explosion is still clear in the landscape, but it has to be recognised.

Likewise it is of more than mere field archaeological interest to be able to recognise medieval ridge and furrow and to distinguish it from seventeenth-century ridging, late eighteenth and early nineteenth-century narrow rig ploughing, seventeenth to nineteenth-century water meadows, nineteenth-century and later land drains and the purely natural phenomenon of stone stripes. All these have played an important part in the physical, social and agricultural history of the areas in which they are found.[11] The ability to see everything in the landscape is therefore the basic and primary requirement of the landscape historian.

Secondly, I would suggest that this type of historian needs a broad background of political, social and economic history as well as a working knowledge of prehistory. This is important, for it is vital to put the results of landscape observation, excavation and documentary research into their correct perspective. Even more important is that such a background helps to avoid the still common fault of many local studies, the parish pump attitude, whereby things are seen in their local setting only. What may be seen as extremely important in a particular parish, whether it is the variety of flint implements of the neolithic period found,[12] the number of moated sites discovered during fieldwork[13] or the drastic effect of plague recorded in an *inquisition post mortem*,[14] may be seen as normal when all these are set in the wider aspect of archaeological studies, fieldwork or economic history.

The third need for total archaeology or landscape history is what geographers would perhaps call 'spatial awareness'. This is the ability to see and understand the relationship of one feature or object to its companions or their relationship to a host of other objects and features which are the preserve of other scholars. This is much more than just the knowledge of map reading and the capacity to make maps. It involves the twin process of recognising patterns and non-patterns both from maps and from the landscape itself. An example of the former is to be able to recognise from the arrangement of parish boundaries which parish has possibly been cut out of another or which joined on to another. This kind of information, which can sometimes be supported by documentary evidence, is of value not only in the minor work of discovering lost medieval settlements, but also in the more important sphere of tracing the layout and development of the early medieval rural landscape.[15] An example of establishing patterns from the landscape itself comes from a study carried out on house typology in Blandford Forum, Dorset. In the almost complete rebuilding of this town after a disastrous fire in 1731, three main types of houses were erected, each with a different room arrangement and thus a different external appearance. These were for shopkeepers, for artisans and for the professional and merchant classes. These houses are not just scattered haphazardly throughout the town, but carefully 'zoned' so that each social class occupied a distinct area of the new town.[16]

Other disciplines

These then are the main requirements for the study of the landscape. However in addition there are others without which it is still not possible to carry out the discipline successfully, even though they are of a lesser order than the first three. One is the need for at least a working knowledge of the basic language and techniques of archaeology. This does not mean necessarily the ability to carry out the excavation of a hill fort, nor the knowledge of the recalibration of carbon-14 dates against the bristlecone pine sequence, but it does involve the understanding of the way 'digging' archaeologists work, the interpretation of their results and especially the validity of the evidence they unearth. All these are very different from the way historians work and interpret their evidence and must be used carefully by the landscape historian if the archaeological evidence is not to be totally misunderstood. This is particularly true in respect of the availability of evidence. The landscape historian, striving to see the origins of a medieval village, might easily use the evidence of a known Roman settlement nearby to show that earlier peoples lived in the same place. But he ought to ask himself if the single Roman settlement was really the only one in his area or, as is much more likely, whether there were many others which no one has ever looked for, let alone discovered. The difficulty of archaeological evidence is that it is always incomplete even at the simple level of distribution. Most so-called archaeological distribution maps are maps of archaeologists only or areas where they have, often sporadically, worked. Areas apparently empty of prehistoric and Roman occupation can only be proved to be truly blank if they have been minutely examined on the ground and from the air over many years with no result and this has never really been achieved.[17]

In addition to this need to understand the work and results of what most people know as archaeology, is the necessity to understand archaeologists of other types, including those whose principal interest is upstanding earthworks and buildings. Here the principles of horizontal and vertical stratigraphy are perhaps the most important. These archaeologists can often decipher the complex development of an Iron Age hill fort without excavation as at Hambledon Hill in Dorset where at least four periods can be recognised.[18] Or they can unravel the accumulated growth of a house, which may have started as a late-medieval aisled

Fig. 2 Barrington, Cambs

photo. Cambridge C.C.

hall, had cross wings added in the fifteenth century, been extended in the sixteenth century and had a ceiling in the hall inserted in the seventeenth century, quite apart from the further additions made even later, which is the history of the building at Barrington illustrated in Fig. 2.[19] The techniques and experience needed to achieve this kind of archaeological sequence are somewhat specialised but the results are extremely important in the wider social history of their respective periods.

Parallel with the need for an archaeological background is that of documentation. By documents, I do not mean just those written on paper or parchment but those carved in stone, including church monuments, gravestones, heraldic devices etc.; and those in the mind, such as folklore and old people's reminiscences. All this involves not just the technical ability to collect and read such documents but fully to understand them and to realise their limitations. The interpretation of Domesday Book, when for example one is concerned with the existence or apparent non-existence of settlements, depends on an understanding of the way in which the information was collected by William the Conqueror's clerks, and the purpose for which this information was meant to be used.[20] Similarly the possible value of late-medieval subsidy rolls has to be set against the known massive evasion and exemption that occurred.[21] Again, to use seventeenth-century inventories, without taking into account the wills that went with them, can result in the most misleading interpretations of the status, wealth and house size of the people involved.[22] The dangers of using old maps and plans also need to be borne in mind. The non-existence of various features on estate, enclosure and tithe maps does not necessarily mean that these were not there at the time the map was made. The purpose for which the map was drawn needs to be known. Thus one does not necessarily expect a map, made to depict visually the land-use of an eighteenth-century estate, to show the existence of a medieval moated site in a copse, even though it was certainly there at that time. In addition it is vital to appreciate that maps, and this includes the various editions of Ordnance Survey maps, were constantly reprinted with very little or no revision often decades after the original survey.[23] Folklore and people's memories, too, though of the greatest value in many respects, can be, and often are, twisted, muddled and altered by later events, attitudes and outlooks and need to be carefully checked and analysed.

Then the student of the landscape needs to be something of an architectural historian in a general sense, that is to be aware of the history and development of design and architectural detail, and to know that the latest fashions in buildings could and did work their way geographically out from certain centres and also down the social scale, both often with a considerable time-lag. For example the concept of the double-depth house with a classical or symmetrical elevation, which arrived in England in the sixteenth century, remained a largely upper-class fashion until the late seventeenth century. It then moved down to the middle levels of society, the parsons, squires and yeomen farmers, reached the smaller tenant farmers by the early nineteenth century and has become ubiquitous in the twentieth century.[24] In an entirely different sphere is the idea of polygonal church towers which appeared in East Anglia by at least the twelfth century. The fashion spread, and, stimulated by the *tour de force* of the Octagon at Ely Cathedral in the fourteenth century, continued until well on into the fifteenth century.[25] Again the introduction of the fashionable 'long gallery' in sixteenth-century great houses is of particular interest, for it caused considerable difficulties in house design and construction for the next eighty years or so, especially when it had to be fitted into buildings which had to have symmetrical elevations at the same time.[26]

Landscape studies also require a background knowledge of a host of other disciplines such as place-names, botany, geology etc.; and specialised techniques such as the interpretation of air-photographs, simple field surveys and the recording of buildings. Space does not permit the writer to go into all these in any detail, except to note that they all need to be understood (not least the techniques of the New Geography and New Archaeology). However, it is worth stressing that it is not necessary to accept absolutely what the specialists of these disciplines and techniques tell us if our own evidence flatly contradicts it. The place-name expert's interpretation of the name Bottisham in Cambridgeshire as 'Boduc's Farm' may be etymologically correct but the earliest form of the name *Bidicheseye*, 'the land by the ditches', is not only topographically an excellent description of the village's situation, but is almost certainly its original name.[27] Likewise the Geological Survey's interpretation of an area of uneven ground north of Rockingham Castle in Northamptonshire as landslip can also be seen to be incorrect. The earthworks are in fact part of the medieval village of Rockingham which later moved to a new site.[28]

Finally the landscape historian must have the ability and broad-mindedness to pick up quickly, use and understand all kinds of techniques and information which are normally beyond the requirements of his field of study. It is difficult to give precise details of what might occur but as an example the writer once had to learn the principles of machine-belt drives so that the scars on the internal walls of an abandoned fenland pumping station could be analysed. This, combined with detailed documentary research, helped towards the drainage history of a piece of the Cambridgeshire landscape.

Integration

The use of all these techniques can ultimately produce a total history of any part of the landscape from the earliest times to the present day, largely of course in the form of a mass of information. The next problem is how to present this material both for the intended reader and the students who have collected and analysed it. For the mere collection of ideas and facts is of no value for scholarship and depressing for the students. It must be assembled into a coherent story that makes sense. The writer's own personal preference, largely due to a geographical training and professional bias, is to reduce as much as possible to a series of chronological maps in order to illustrate the history of the landscape visually.[29] Even this has to be supported by a written account with detailed plans of sites and houses where necessary, and photographs where possible. This, like much else in this paper, is an ideal probably never to be actually achieved, but it is worth aiming for whether the area of study is a single parish or a large geographical unit.

The methods of work and the results of total archaeology, within the framework of adult education teaching, are of considerable academic value for special reasons. For one thing, most scholars, in the present-day academic rat-race, can neither afford time, nor are they prepared to spend time in carrying out the detailed fieldwork and often simple, but time-consuming, documentary work that good total archaeology requires. Yet this is just the kind of work that can be successfully achieved by groups of adult education students with a careful division of labour, as Victor Skipp has pointed out in a slightly different context.[30]

However, total archaeology has a far more important use in the wider field of education. In any area, a group of students working in the way I have suggested may be dealing with aspects of geology, natural history, social and economic history, archaeology etc., and even at times political and constitutional history, as well as many other related studies. This is education in the broadest sense which I believe we desperately need in our specialised age. In addition such work is also vital in widening the interest in, and appreciation of, our total environment at a time when modern developments, technology and over-population threaten to destroy both it and us. By making adult education students aware of the history of their environment it is just possible that they will be able to play some part in the decisions on its future. With luck and effort by these students it may be that enough of it will be protected and conserved for the pleasure and education of future generations.

Notes

1 D. Portman, *Exeter Houses, 1400–1700* (1966).
2 W. Ison, *The Georgian Buildings of Bath* (1949).
3 D. Ward, 'The pre-urban cadaster and the urban pattern of Leeds', *Annals of Ass. American Geog.* 52 (1962) pp. 150–66; H. J. Dyos, *A Victorian Suburb* (1961).
4 C. C. Taylor, 'Whiteparish: a study in the development of a forest edge parish', *Wilts. Archaeol. Mag.* 62 (1967) pp. 86–91.
5 C. C. Taylor, 'Medieval and later field shapes in Dorset', *Procs. Dorset Nat. Hist. and Archaeol. Soc.* 90 (1969) pp. 249–57.
6 A. Raistrick, *West Riding of Yorkshire* (1970) pp. 71–5.
7 W. G. Hoskins, *Leicestershire* (1957) pp. 90–4.
8 C. C. Taylor, *The Making of the Cambridgeshire Landscape* (1973).
9 C. C. Taylor, *Dorset* (1970) pp. 169–70.
10 P. Eden, 'Smaller post-medieval houses in eastern England', in *East Anglian Studies*, ed. L. M. Munby (1968) pp. 71–93.
11 H. C. Bowen, *Ancient Fields* (1961).
12 C. Fox, *The Archaeology of the Cambridge Region* (1923).
13 C. C. Taylor, 'Moated sites in Cambridgeshire', in *Archaeology and the Landscape*, ed. P. J. Fowler (1972) pp. 237–48.
14 M. Spufford, *A Cambridgeshire Community* (1965) pp. 31–2.
15 C. D. Drew, 'The manors of the Iwerne Valley', *Procs. Dorset Archaeol. Soc.* 69 (1948) pp. 45–50.
16 R.C.H.M., *Dorset* III (1970) pp. 16–19.
17 C. C. Taylor, 'The study of settlement patterns in pre-Saxon Britain', in *Man, Settlement and Urbanism*, ed. P. J. Ucko *et al.* (1972) pp. 109–13.

18 R.C.H.M., *Dorset* III (1970), Child Okeford (22).

19 R.C.H.M., *West Cambridgeshire* (1968), Barrington (17).

20 V. H. Galbraith, *The Making of Domesday Book* (1961); W. G. Hoskins, 'The highland zone in Domesday Book', in *Provincial England* (1963) pp. 15–52.

21 E. M. Yates, 'Medieval assessments in north-west Sussex', *Trans. Inst. Brit. Geographers*, 23 (1954) pp. 75–92; J. B. D. Sheail, '1525 Lay Subsidy Returns', unpublished Ph.D. thesis, London University (1968).

22 D. G. Vaisey, 'Probate inventories of Lichfield and district, 1568–1680' *Hist. Coll. Staffs.*, 5 (1969) pp. 3–5.

23 J. B. Harley, *The Historian's Guide to Ordnance Survey Maps* (1964); J. B. Harley, 'Christopher Greenwood, county map-maker', *J. Worcestershire Hist. Soc.* (1962) pp. 41–54.

24 C. C. Taylor, *Dorset* (1970) pp. 146–8.

25 T. D. Atkinson, 'Local character in the ancient architecture of Cambridgeshire', *Procs. Cambs. Ant. Soc.* 40 (1944) pp. 34–6.

26 R.C.H.M., *Dorset* II Pt 2 (1970), Warmwell (2); *West Cambridgeshire* (1968), Madingley (2).

27 P. H. Reaney, *The Place Names of Cambridgeshire* (1943) pp. 129–30; C. R. Hart, *The Early Charters of Eastern England* (1966) pp. 50–1.

28 Geol. Survey. One inch map sheet No. 171.

29 C. C. Taylor, 'Whiteparish: a study in the development of a forest edge parish', *Wilts. Archaeol. Mag.*, 62 (1967) pp. 79–102; 'Three deserted medieval settlements in Whiteparish, *Wilts. Archaeol. Mag.*, 63 (1968) pp. 39–45; R.C.H.M., *North-East Cambridgeshire* (1972) liv–lxv.

30 V. H. T. Skipp, 'The place of team work in local history', in *Local History*, ed. H. P. R. Finberg and V. H. T. Skipp (1967) pp. 87–102.

Parliamentary enclosure and the documents for its study

Rex C. Russell, *Staff Tutor in Local Studies in the Department of Adult Education at the University of Hull, has worked for several years with his adult classes on parliamentary enclosure in north Lincolnshire. The results of his studies have been published in a number of booklets. In this paper he discusses the way in which the study of the documents of enclosure and of the landscape are essentially part of the same process of recovering the past.*

This paper begins by listing the essential sources which make possible a local enclosure study; it continues with mention of further documentary records which it is desirable to use if they are available, and it indicates briefly the content and use of each document mentioned.

What are the absolutely essential sources? They are these three:

1. *The enclosure award* (the permanent legal record of the enclosure) together with the surveyor's map which is an integral part of the award.
2. *The modern six-inch Ordnance Survey maps* of the district under study; one needs sufficient sheets to cover not only the parish under study but also lands outside the parish boundaries.
3. *The landscape* of the parish and its neighbours (not forgetting the buildings which lie within the landscape and form an essential feature of it).

One cannot make any adequate study of a local enclosure without using these three basic records; the landscape must be used, not merely seen, as one of the indispensable sources.

What are the other sources which it is desirable, but not absolutely essential to use, if they are available? It is convenient to list these, noticing that the first three are usually much more easily available than the others.

(*a*) The local enclosure Act: many copies of each Act were printed.

(*b*) The notices of intended enclosure in the relevant county newspaper.

(*c*) The enclosure commissioners' notices of their meetings held between the date of the passing of the Act and that of the execution of their award. These normally appear in the county newspaper, inserted frequently during the earlier months and less often as the enclosure draws to completion.

(*d*) The minutes of these commissioners' meetings.

(*e*) The accounts of the costs of enclosure.

(*f*) Any letters concerning the enclosure, any notes made by the clerk to the commissioners; papers dealing with negotiations for the extinguishment of tithe; rights of warren and any other rights to be compensated for at enclosure; any documents containing such details as the course of husbandry to be followed in the parish during enclosure; possible future warping proposals; instructions for drainage, embanking and hedging and fencing.

There may remain, to give further examples, notices relating to the sales of land during enclosure; lists of the claims submitted by the owners of land and owners of rights of common together with papers dealing with any objections to such claims and with the outcome of such objections; notices dealing with existing roads and footways which are to be stopped up at enclosure, together with plans of proposed new roads to be laid out.

If these records do survive (and the offices of local solicitors have been known to house such collections) then their examination and use can obviously enable us to obtain much more detailed information on any local enclosure. However, a perfectly adequate study can result from an intelligent use of the three essential documents first mentioned. What information do they contain and how can this be used?

The enclosure award

An award begins with a summary of the main provisions of the local Act: for this reason, if we fail to find a copy of the Act itself we are not seriously hindered. The main body of the award lists and describes the courses of all the new public and private roads and footways together with their dimensions. The courses and detailed dimensions of public and private drains and watercourses are similarly listed, together with instructions for their regular future cleansing and maintenance. The *special allotments* are next described: these are the lands awarded in lieu of manorial rights, rights of warren (where these existed), the parson's glebe and common rights; the lands (or corn-rents) awarded in lieu of great and small tithes (where such awards were made); the lands

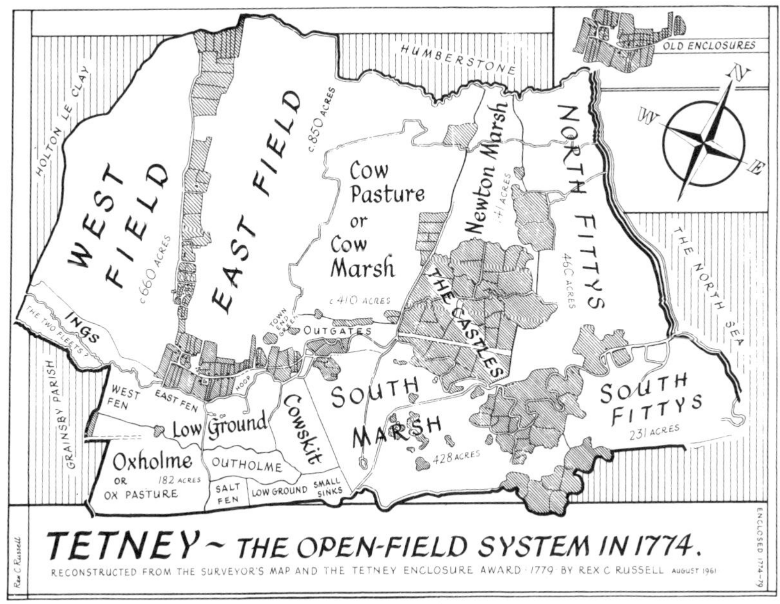

Fig. 3a Tetney—open field system in 1774

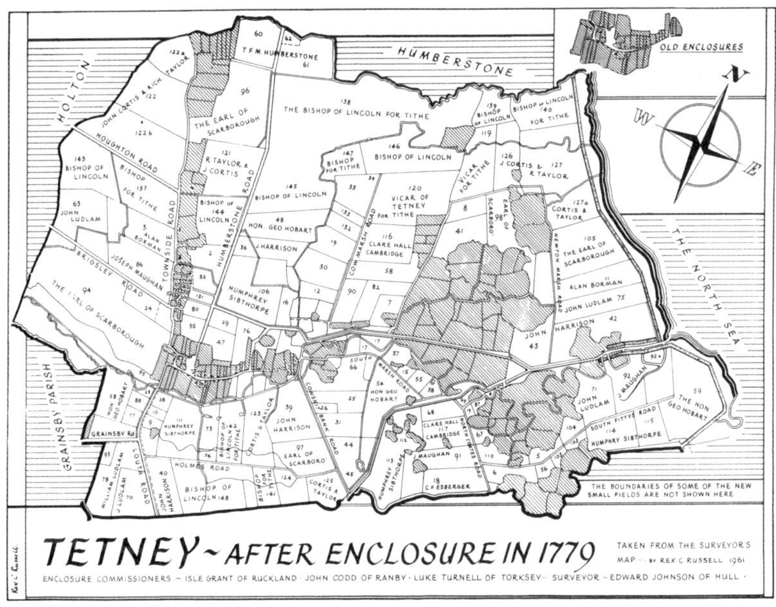

Fig. 3b Tetney – after enclosure in 1779

awarded to the parish surveyors of the highways for the digging of chalk, stone, sand and gravel for the maintenance of the parish roads and occasionally for other parish needs. The great bulk of most awards is concerned with the allocation of the *general allotments* of land awarded in lieu of former holdings in the open fields and of former rights of common. Each separate plot is described, its ownership is given together with its acreage and (in the vast majority of cases) its location *in terms of its position in the open fields, commons or waste grounds*. Exchanges of lands and of old enclosures are normally recorded and one may glean valuable information from the *names* of closes which are given to aid identification. The awards usually end with specific instructions for fencing, hedging and drainage. Occasionally, but too infrequently for the satisfaction of the student, there are details of the total costs of enclosure and a share of these costs is assigned to each of the owners of the general allotments.

We can thus obtain from the award a complete list of all persons and institutions receiving land at enclosure, together with the locations and acreages of each of the plots which they were awarded. The surveyor's map depicts, in detail, the post-enclosure plan of the parish with the lines of the new hedges or fences, drains, roads, road-pits and other new features. Using these two classes of information together it is possible to reconstruct the earlier open field pattern. Normally the surveyor's map will show clearly the old enclosures, the stopped-up roads and sometimes the positions of village buildings, while occasionally the boundaries of the former commons and open fields may also be seen. We can thus reconstruct maps of the parish immediately before and after enclosure, using information from the surveyor's map and the enclosure award (Figs 3a and 3b).

The modern six-inch Ordnance Survey map

We can turn now to our second essential document, the modern six-inch Ordnance Survey map of the parish and its neighbours. It is invariably informative and revealing to superimpose on this map (using coloured inks which do not obliterate the names and features on the printed sheets) the open field pattern. It is easiest to begin by marking in (usually in green) the old enclosures, for these are often the one enduring feature: time and time again the old closes shown on the surveyor's map of 1780 or 1798, 1812 or 1833 are unchanged in shape on the modern OS maps. Some new enclosure roads may well have become disused footpaths but the old enclosures have a remarkable permanency. What is gained by this superimposition of a former open field pattern on the modern OS map? It helps to reveal, quite vividly, the logic of the open field system, and of former land use within the parish. One can see clearly why the open fields, the ings, the common pastures and the sykes were in their particular situations.[1] The logic of this layout becomes apparent even if we do not yet know this particular parish on the ground. It also helps us to appreciate how rarely it was possible for the commissioners to award new blocks of land in ring fences (unless very *few* owners were given land). Farm lands after enclosure usually remain dispersed, but in larger units than before; each of the new owners needed land in different situations within the parish for varying agricultural uses. The locations of outlying post-enclosure farmsteads and other buildings, and perhaps former farm land now put to alternative use also become apparent from these maps.

One of the things which becomes clear when such a study is made over a number of adjacent parishes, is that enclosure was normally a parish-by-parish process, with the re-planning stopping at each boundary. An enclosure Act normally empowered enclosure within a single parish (or part of that parish); it is rare to find an Act authorising the enclosure of two adjoining parishes. One set of commissioners enclosed parish A in, for example, 1793–6; another set of commissioners may have enclosed the adjoining parish B thirty years later, while parish C may have been enclosed by agreement in 1617, each implementing different ideas and producing different road plans and field patterns. Roads laid out in one parish may thus stop at the boundary and lead nowhere! More frequently, roads change both their direction and width at parish boundaries. Similarly, the field patterns of adjacent parishes may bear no relation at all to that within the parish we are studying. One parish may have been divided into a few large fields because, at enclosure, land within it had been owned by few people, while over the boundary in the adjoining parish there may be a multitude of small closes because many small owners there were awarded land. On one side of the boundary one group of commissioners may have laid out the new fields with their dividing hedges running parallel with that boundary, whilst in the next parish another group of commissioners may well have planned their new fields with hedges at right angles to that boundary (Fig. 4).

These facts may be apparent from the map; they must be checked and further information must be sought from the third of our three essential sources, the landscape itself.

The landscape

There are two purposeful approaches to the use of landscape as our third record. One can begin, on the ground, by asking questions about different aspects of the appearance of fields, hedgerows, drains, footpaths, roads, pits and of the buildings in the landscape and then follow up these questions by attempting to answer them through the use of the two other sources already mentioned—the OS map and the enclosure

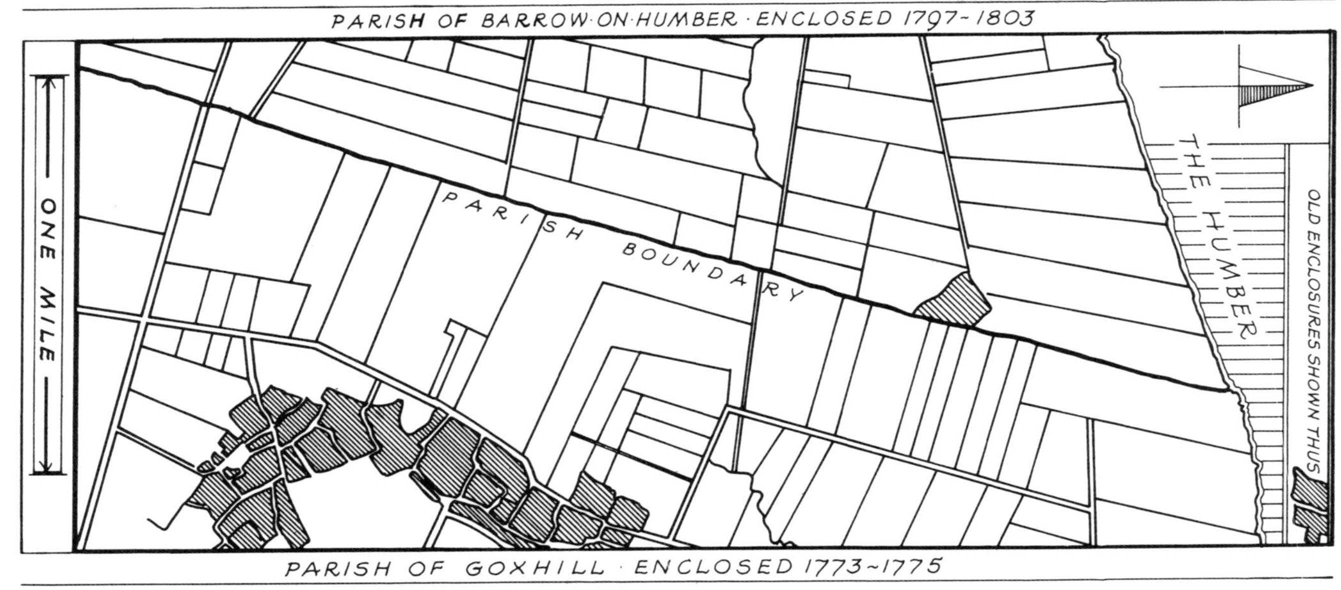

Fig. 4 Field changes at a parish boundary: Goxhill and Barrow-on-Humber

award with its map. Alternatively, one can use the information gleaned from the award and the six-inch map and go out to check on the ground facts we have gathered indoors from these sources, together with questions these sources have raised. One approach clearly complements the other: we need to use both.

Perhaps the clearest way of indicating briefly how to start with the landscape itself is to list some of the questions arising. Why does this wide road with broad grass verges turn abruptly at this point, and why do the verges narrow considerably and virtually disappear? Why is this lane now slightly higher than the fields on each side of it and further on sunk well below the level of the adjoining closes? Why do these particular hedges enclose an irregularly shaped field whilst those hedges are straight, enclosing rectangular fields at right-angles to the road? What can explain the fact that this hedge, set upon a noticeable bank, runs an irregular course for several miles although the fields which abut on to it on either side are markedly regular in shape, with straight hedges? What was the purpose of this disused road-pit? Why do I find in *this* hedge holly, blackthorn, hedge maple, ash and whitethorn, whilst I can discover in *that* hedge only two species of hedgerow timber, elder and whitethorn? Why is this farmstead, well away from the village, built mainly of chalk (or limestone), whilst the great majority of these farms are brick built? Why is this straight road, about sixty feet wide, only a wide grass track and why does it end at this hedge? Why, in this ploughed field, do I see across its whole width alternate wide strips of lighter and darker soil? And why, across this field, has the grass turned yellowy-brown in a broad band running diagonally through green grass? Why does this farmer clean out that ditch which is outside his boundary hedge? Why do these two adjacent brick-pit ponds have a hedge and bank dividing them?

Such queries are all meaningful: they are not, of course, the only questions which landscape can prompt. To use the landscape like a document we must ask questions of what is visible; as the landscapes change, so too will the questions we ask. (It is advisable to write these down as they are prompted by what is seen.)

If we use as our starting points the enclosure award and the OS map it is also worthwhile to begin by making a written list of the questions which they prompt and to which we hope the landscape will suggest answers. Some of the relevant queries could be these which follow: it is important to ask them even though we may be unsatisfied with the tentative conclusions we reach. What are the building materials of the post-enclosure farms and cottages? Where did this material come from? Are the outlying farms of similar date or of widely different dates? (The first editions of the one-inch OS maps are useful in establishing which farmsteads were in existence by the date of the survey.) If chalk or limestone were used for the building of some of these farmsteads, where was it quarried? (In some Lincolnshire parishes, Wootton and Barton on Humber for example, chalk was the main building material for the earlier post-enclosure farms and the sites of the quarries are adjacent to these new farmsteads.) If the new farms are of brick, is there any evidence for the digging of clay and the burning of bricks near the site? These activities were not particularly unusual; in isolated areas and at a period before a local brick and tile industry had been established, these practices were probably more widespread than is commonly recognised.[2] If not, where did the bricks come from? Are they of the normal local colour or do they stand out as being quite different? Is there evidence that post-enclosure building, combined with the growing local population, led to the establishment of short-lived local brick and tile making? Have all the awarded roads been metalled, and are they still in use? Have all the awarded road-pit plots in fact been used for digging or quarrying road materials? What are the main hedging quicksets? Are the post-enclosure hedges over the former open fields markedly different from those which divide the former moors and commons? Have ditches been used as field boundaries in the low-lying areas instead of hedges? Are the hedges of the old enclosures visibly different from those sub-dividing the former open lands? Are there many more species of hedgerow timbers in the old enclosures than in the post-enclosure boundaries? Is ridge and furrow still visible? How does it run, *through* hedges and across roads or only *within* hedged closes? Are the former farmsteads within the village old enclosures still identifiable even though no longer used as farms? Have new public roads (other than those on modern building estates), not planned and awarded by the commissioners, been laid out after enclosure? Have post-enclosure developments occurred *within* plots awarded at enclosure? Has the shape and size of these awarded plots limited the extent of such developments? (At Barton on Humber, it is noticeable that the digging of clay for local brick and tile making normally occurred within such plots, the hedged boundaries remaining between the now disused brick ponds in many cases.) Has there been sub-division of the larger plots awarded at enclosure? If so, are the resulting hedging quicksets different from those of the fields designed by the commissioners? What are the main differences in the landscapes of two or three adjoining parishes? How many of these variations can be accounted for by enclosure?

It will be obvious that another class of record—air photographs—can be most profitably used in conjunction with maps and landscapes: these may be particularly valuable in those parishes in which modern farming practice has recently removed large numbers of hedges or bulldozed and ploughed the old enclosures on the outskirts of a village.[3]

Other sources

Now that the use of our three essential sources has been indicated, we can consider the worth and use of the valuable but inessential documents already listed.

First, let us discuss the *commissioners' notices* of their meetings held during the course of enclosure. These notices provide a timetable of enclosure, a dated sequence of events between the passing of the local Act and the completion of enclosure with the execution of the award. Such information is useful if, as is too often the case, no commissioners' minutes exist. The notices in the county newspaper reveal the dates and purposes of the commissioners' meetings, when claims (to land and common rights) must be delivered, when the road system was designed and advertised, when the fencing of the tithe allotments and the stoning of the roads was to be carried out, and at what date the owners of awarded land could receive a schedule of the sizes and positions of their plots.[4] In addition to such a timetable, the notices themselves may contain other useful facts, for example (*a*) notices of the sale of land during enclosure, sometimes in order to raise money to meet part of the expenses incurred; (*b*) notices to contractors inviting tenders for different works—for making bridges, cutting drains, fencing the tithe allotments, stoning the new roads, '. . . the work to be done according to the following specifications, with Cliff stone, 13 feet wide and 10 inches thick, and then to be covered, 11 feet wide and four inches thick, with the middle-sized spurn gravel; . . .' (Scotter (Lincs) enclosure, 1811); (*c*) advertisements for labour and for quicksets for the new hedges: 'A number of workmen wanted to complete the works upon the said Inclosure; application to be made to the Agent upon the work. Also wanted, 300,000 good 3 feet Ash Plants, and 500,000 good strong Quick . . .' (Ulceby (Lincs) enclosure, 1824). The search for commissioners' notices in the county newspaper may well result in the finding of other relevant information. The enclosure of Helpstone (Northants) commenced in June 1809 and its results were mourned by John Clare:

> Enclosure like a Buonaparte let not a thing remain,
> It levelled every bush and tree and levelled every hill
> And hung the moles for traitors—though the brook is running still
> It runs a naked stream, cold and chill . . .

One reason for Clare's anger, and one cause of the stream's nakedness, can be gleaned from the following notice overleaf in the *Stamford Mercury*, 18 October 1811.

WILLOWS

To be SOLD by AUCTION

On Tuesday, the 29th day of October, 1811, . . . at the EARL OF EXETER'S ARMS at HELPSTONE: ABOUT 1450 WILLOW TREES, in 60 lots, the most part fit to saw into boards and rails, and the greatest part with very fine tops which will split into rails, the remainder fit for hurdles; and a few thriving Ash Trees, some Ash Pollards, and Firewood, now growing in HELPSTONE FIELDS, and which are to be taken down on account of the inclosure . . .

Notices of *Intended Inclosure* which appear in the county newspaper are worth searching for in the months prior to the date of the passing of the local Act. The Act for the enclosure of Louth was passed in June 1801. Notices for this appeared in the *Stamford Mercury* in issues of 20 March, 17 April and 1 May 1801 (and earlier in the same newspaper, in 1796 on the 19 August and 9 September). The notice in the paper of 20 March 1801 reads:

INCLOSURE OF LOUTH FIELDS

A MEETING of the Proprietors of Estates in the Parish of Louth . . . will be held at the BRICKLAYERS' ARMS INN, in LOUTH . . . on THURSDAY the 9th day of April next, at 10 o'clock in the Forenoon, to adjust the claim of the Lords of the Manor, appoint Commissioners and a Surveyor, and read over, settle, and sign the Draft of the Bill intended to be presented to Parliament, in the present Session, for dividing and inclosing the open and common Fields, and other open and commonable Lands in the said Parish; at which Meeting all Persons interested are requested to attend.

By Order, ROB. PADDISON

The main value of such series of notices of intended enclosure is not to the student studying *one* particular parish enclosure, but to the researcher making a study of enclosure over a county or part of a county. In the latter case a collection of such notices reveals in many cases that long delays occurred between the first public discussion of intended enclosures and the final passing of the local Acts. Such information can usually be obtained only from the county newspapers. Examples of such delays (in Lincolnshire) are as follows:

Parish	*Newspaper notice of intended enclosure*	*Date of the enclosure Act*
Scotter	1795	1808
N. Kelsey	1795	1812
Ulceby	1801	1824
Fulstow	1801	1817
N. Thoresby	1801	1836 (General Act)
Scunthorpe and Frodingham	1812	1831

The use of the third of our inessential documents, the printed local enclosure *Act*, may now be indicated. We have noted that its main contents will have been summarised in the preamble of the award, but if a copy of the Act is available it should be used. If we use the Act with a series of questions in mind we will be able to make profitable use of the facts it may provide.

Such queries could be as follows. What rates of payment does the Act authorise for the commissioners and the surveyor or surveyors? Does the Act include safeguards concerning the expenses of enclosure—have the commissioners to present accounts quarterly for the inspection of local JPs? Who is empowered to nominate new commissioners in the event of the death or refusal to serve of those named in the Act (this information helps us to ascertain who originally chose each of the commissioners)? What is to happen to copyhold tenants and to other tenant farmers? Are there clauses which protect tenants' interests in any way, or provisions which safeguard the claims of common-right owners? Does the Act recite what is to happen to squatters? Are provisions made for compensation for the extinguishment of rights of warren and for the destruction of rabbits? What, if any, are the contents of the clauses dealing with granting land (or corn-rents) in lieu of great and small tithes? What proportions of the open fields, the commons and the waste grounds are to be awarded in lieu of future tithes? Are the old enclosures to remain titheable? If tithes are to be extinguished on the old enclosures, what is to happen to persons who own only old enclosures? Does the Act provide a right of appeal to the JPs in Quarter Sessions against commissioners' decisions? Are there detailed clauses concerning warping of land after enclosure?

Different Acts will prompt different questions, and although many of them follow a common pattern, there will always be some provisions in one particular Act which others will not contain; these should always be noted.

It is difficult and perhaps unnecessary to attempt to summarise the contents and to indicate the use of the remaining sources. The minutes of the commissioners' meetings record decisions made, but rarely give the evidence on which they were based: they certainly amplify the details in the timetable of a particular enclosure,[5] and they reveal the frequency of attendance of particular commissioners. In some cases valuable details of the agricultural use of land in the parish appear in these minutes, and one may find here apportioned costs of enclosure. These costs may be detailed amongst the clerk to the commissioners' papers (which may well exist in solicitors' offices today). The value of such costs can best be appreciated from the actual specimens which follow (all from parishes in Lincolnshire):

Parish, with dates of enclosure	*Acreage enclosed*	*Cost* £ s d	*Cost per acre* £ s d
Barnetby le Wold 1766–1768	*c.* 2,260	1,400 13 1	12 4½
Kirmington 1777–1778	*c.* 1,643	1,285 9 5	15 7½
Kirton Lindsey 1793–1801	*c.* 4,325	5,267 16 0	1 4 4
Hibaldstow 1796–1803	*c.* 4,233	8,243 2 3½	1 18 11
Wrawby cum Brigg 1800–1805	*c.* 2,976	4,950 2 10	1 13 3

This second table indicates how the total cost was made up.

The main items of costs	*Parishes in north Lincolnshire* *Barrow on Humber* £	s	d	*N. Kelsey* £	s	d	*Hibaldstow* £	s	d
Solicitors' and parliamentary expenses	1,174	5	7	4,013	13	0[a]	1,301	5	7
Surveyor	796	10	0	210	0	0	1,043	7	6
Commissioners	926	13	7	1,780	0	0	753	10	4
Drains	1,500	7	11				1,097	12	7
Embankments	3,643	8	11[b]				667	5	4
Tithe allotments fencing	1,498	16	1	4,985	10	1	1,283	0	2
Roads	4,465	9	10				1,364	9	2
Bridges	287	3	0				394	0	7
Incidents	159	8	1	1,505	1	0	338	11	0½

(The N. Kelsey figure of £4,985 10s 1d is bracketed against Drains, Embankments, Tithe allotments fencing, Roads and Bridges.)

[a] Included here are these items:

Parliamentary fees	£712	19	2
Solicitors' bills	£1,943	0	9
Clerks to the commissioners	£1,357	13	1

[b] Included are the costs of jetties, cloughs and the Humber banks.

This chapter has attempted to deal with the essential documents which make possible a local enclosure study, together with some of the valuable but less important sources which a student should attempt to locate and examine. Enclosure can make a satisfying and rewarding study for the student of local history. Whilst such a study must deal with one parish at a time (for most enclosures were of single parishes), greater satisfaction and deeper insights into the problems of parliamentary enclosure can be obtained from examining and mapping the enclosures of a group of adjoining parishes. Such research can help to reveal the logic of the separate open field systems, and the various ways in which they helped to solve the agricultural problems posed to the farming communities by the different geography of their separate parishes. Fig. 5 depicts three Lincolnshire parishes (unusually large ones) fronting on the Humber and reaching inland to the Wolds: each of these parishes evolved a logical open field system which made good use of geographical differences between them.

Notes

1 'Ings'—meadowland: (a crop of hay was taken off before beasts were allowed in to graze). 'Sykes'—narrow strips of meadow normally bordering a stream.

2 A notice addressed to builders, specifying conditions of contract for the building of Ruckland Rectory (a remote wold parish) ends with this sentence: 'The Contractor will have the privilege of making his own Bricks for the Works on hand immediately contiguous to the site'. (*Stamford Mercury* 7 December 1835).

3 The use of air photographs cannot be developed in this chapter. A most valuable guide to their use is M. W. Beresford and J. K. S. St Joseph, *Medieval England, An Aerial Survey* (1958).

4 Examples of such notices together with their use may be seen in Rex C. Russell, *The Enclosures of Market Rasen 1779–1781 and of Wrawby cum Brigg 1800–1805* (published by Market Rasen W.E.A. 1969), and Rex C. Russell, *The Enclosures of Scawby 1770–1771, Kirton in Lindsey 1793–1801, and Hibaldstow 1796–1803* (Barton on Humber W.E.A., 1970).

5 See for example the summary of commissioners' minutes for the enclosure of Ashby (near Scunthorpe, Lincs.) between 1801 and 1809 in Rex C. Russell, 'The enclosures of Bottesford and Yaddlethorpe 1794–97, Messingham 1798–1804 and Ashby 1801–09' (*Journal of Scunthorpe Museum Society*, Vol. 1, No. 1 1964), or a similar summary of the commissioners' minutes for Scartho enclosure 1795–98, in Gillett, Russell and Trevitt, *The Enclosures of Scartho 1795–1798 and Grimsby 1827–1840* (published by Grimsby Public Libraries and Museum, second edition 1970).

Historical ecology

Max Hooper, *a member of the staff of the Nature Conservancy's Monks Wood Experimental Station, Huntingdon, develops further his pioneering studies of hedgerows and their shrub contents which may help to establish their dates and early nature. The argument over this technique of analysing field remains continues, and few people state the case for hedgerow dating more strongly than Dr Hooper: 'although ecologists can gain much from historical evidence, historians will gain even more from ecological evidence'. The paper provides one detailed example of the need for the historian to use all types of sources available, both in the landscapes and in the documents.*

Although both words in the title are very familiar, their use in conjunction may appear a little bizarre, especially since ecology has become, in the popular press, synonymous with both pollution and conservation. It seems proper, therefore, to begin with a formal definition. Ecology is a branch of science which deals with the interrelationships between organisms and their environments and attempts to explain spatial distribution of species. History, as I understand it, is the art of interpreting man's past activities. Historical ecology is therefore the art, science, craft or mystery of elucidating these present patterns of organisms in the light of man's past activities.

Ecology has formerly been concerned with explanations of spatial distribution patterns in terms of climate, soil or mutual interactions between species. The new historical ecologists recognise what is obvious, that *homo sapiens* is the dominant species, and therefore the interaction between man and other organisms is of major importance. This has been realised by others in the past, but it is only in the last five or six years that a group of ecologists has migrated as a matter of course from the field in summer to the record office in winter.

The first paper published which really used historical documentation in a systematic way in order to explain the distribution of plants in woods was by Dr Rackham on Cambridgeshire coppices.[1] Mr Tubbs' book *The New Forest: an Ecological History* was published in 1968, and it was followed in 1969 by a third woodland study, by Dr Peterken, which deals with Staverton Park in Suffolk.[2] Work on the historical ecology of grasslands dates back to 1968, with Mr Wells' use of various documents to explain declines in the pasque flower over the past one hundred and fifty years.[3] This was quickly followed in 1969 by more grassland studies, notably in the *Monks Wood Symposium* No. 5 on 'Old Grassland'.[4] The first meeting of an informal group of ecologists and historians—The Historical Ecology Discussion Group—also took place in 1969, and has met regularly at Monks Wood ever since.

Hedges and dating

In retrospect 1969 seems to have been a vintage year, for also in that year and again at Monks Wood a conference on my own speciality, 'Hedges and Local History', was organised jointly by the Botanical Society of the British Isles and the Standing Conference for Local History, resulting in the publication of the booklet *Hedges and Local History* (1970). This work on hedges is slightly different from the main stream of historical ecology. Hitherto we have attempted to use documents to demonstrate a causal relationship between man's past activities and a current spatial distribution of plants. The work on hedges began like this: as an ecologist I believed that the older a hedge was, the earlier it was planted and the longer it had been managed as a boundary, then the more shrub species it would have in it. So I examined documents in order to date the creation of specific hedges which could be examined at the present time. I managed to assign dates from documents to 227 hedges in various parts of lowland England and then visited each one and counted the shrub species present in 30-yard lengths. The correlation between the age of the hedge and the number of shrub species in this length was very good: the correlation coefficient (r) came to 0·85, but it is also possible to go further and calculate a regression equation to predict the age of a hedge from the number of species in it:

$$\text{age of hedge in years} = (\text{number of species} \times 110) + 30$$

Using this equation, a hedge with two species would be 250 years old and a ten-species hedge would be 1,130 years old. One can also calculate the degree of error likely and it is probably better to state that in nineteen cases out of twenty a hedge with ten species in it is between 940 and 1,320 years old.

The hedges used here came from various places across the country and it seemed possible that this large error could be reduced by examining smaller areas. As a test case I used the clay uplands on the border

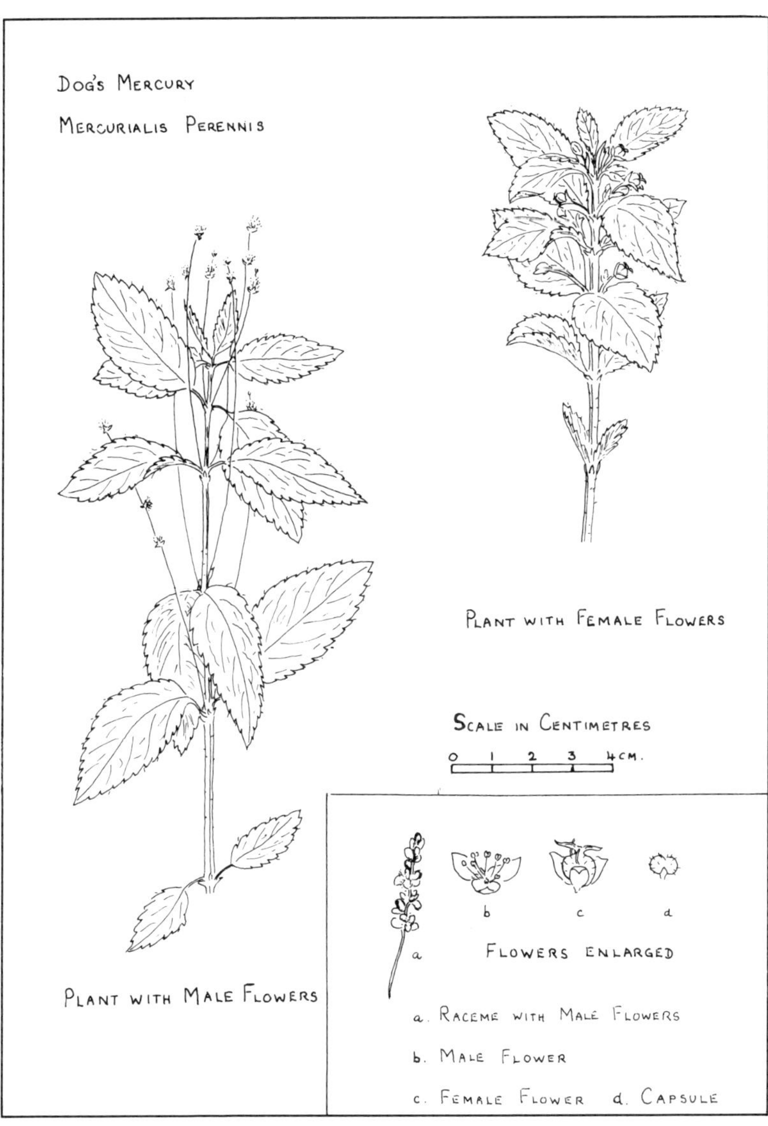

Fig. 5 Dog's mercury

between Huntingdonshire and Northamptonshire. Here I found 95 hedges which could be dated from documents. The correlation coefficient (r) came to 0·92 and the regression equation for predicting the age of a hedge from a shrub count in this area came to

$$\text{age of hedge in years} = (99 \times \text{number of species}) - 16$$

Now it is as well to be clear how this hedgerow work differs from that of some other historical ecologists. The first part is essentially similar: documents are used to demonstrate that species-rich hedges are older than species-poor ones. This does not differ from a demonstration from documents that the woods in which the oxlip (*Primula elatior*) occurs are all ancient woodlands. These both fall within the formal definition of explaining spatial distribution by means of the historical record. But in calculating an equation to predict the age of a hedge from a count of shrubs I am implying that one can reverse the process. This may appear to be a circular argument and may have some logical deficiencies. For example, having found the oxlip in ten woods known to be ancient it is reasonable to suppose that the eleventh wood in which it is found is also ancient. It is however unreasonable, on the evidence thus stated, to say that the absence of the oxlip from the eleventh wood implies a more recent origin for that wood. Only if one had documentary evidence for the date of origin of a number of woodlands from which the oxlip was absent as well as present could one calculate a correlation and hence make a prediction about the history of an undocumented wood from the plants growing in it.

Hedges and woodland

'Hooper's hedgerow hypothesis'[5] was, I think, the first step in this direction but alongside this we must now put 'Pollard's postulate'. Put as succinctly as possible, Dr Pollard postulates that hedges cut out of woodland, or assart hedges, can be recognised today by certain constituents of their ground flora, notably bluebells, wood anemones and dog's mercury[6] (Fig. 5).

The crucial piece of evidence that Dr Pollard found concerns a hedge at Monks Wood. The first document in the case is a recent aerial photograph which shows that a section of the hedge has been realigned. The second is an OS map of 1835 which shows the realignment in existence then. The third is the Alconbury Weston Inclosure Award Map of 1791 which shows the old boundary. The realignment therefore took place between 1791 and 1835.

The fourth document is an estate map of 1612 which shows Monks Wood abutting onto the old hedge line. So some time between 1612 and 1791 the fields on the south edge of Monks Wood were 'assarted'. Note that this woodland clearance took place before the new hedge was planted.

The final document in this sequence is the attestation of Alexander Maufe to the Sawtry Abbey foundation charter of 1147 in which the boundary of the abbey estate runs 'just where the Countess Judith put a hedge around the wood'. This lady was William the Conqueror's niece who came into the estate when her husband was executed for treason (AD 1075), so that the old hedge may be about 900 years old. Indeed it may be older, as it was a hundred boundary and is still a parish boundary.

Thus there are five sections in the hedge, A, B, C, D and E (Fig. 6) of which A and E are old (say 900 years) and B, C and D are young (150 years). Using Hooper's hedgerow hypothesis parts A and E should have nine species of shrub, and lengths taken at random do give eight, nine or ten species. Sections B, C and D should have two species but in fact usually have three species. Perhaps it was planted as a two-species hedge with ash and hawthorn?

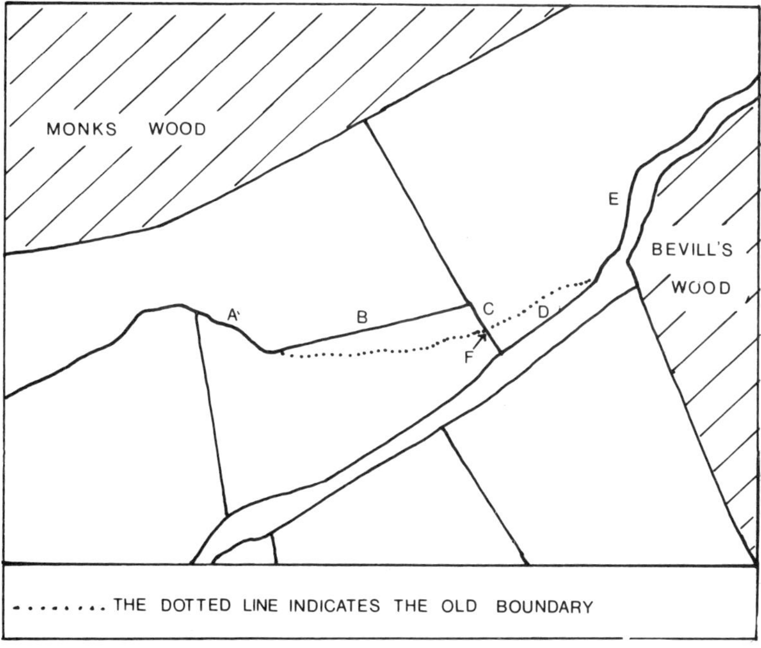

Fig. 6 Monk's wood (old boundaries)

If Pollard's postulate is correct, Sections A and E should have in them the woodland herbs such as bluebell, wood anemone and dog's mercury —and they do; sections B, C and D should not have them—and they don't. At least, there is some dog's mercury in section C but this is precisely on the old hedge line (at point F)!

Dr Pollard has a lot more evidence for Huntingdonshire assarts and I for one now take the presence of dog's mercury in a Huntingdonshire hedge as pretty good evidence for former woodland.

To some extent this belief is reinforced by the biology of the species. dog's mercury (*mercurialis perennis*) is a hairy, creeping perennial, with unbranched stems.* It has dark green, toothed leaves in opposite pairs, and small green flowers without petals. The plant has separate male and female plants. The male flowers grow in long racemes, on separate plants from the female flowers, which are hidden among the leaves. At first the plants are quite short—four to six inches high when the flowers begin to come—but they lengthen considerably as the season wears on. The male plant shown in Figure 5 depicts the lengthening stem and racemes by about April; the female plant is shown at an earlier stage. The normal flowering period is from February or March to May.

The male and female plants do not always grow in the same district. Further, the female bears relatively few seeds (*c.* 300), of which only 5 per cent to 10 per cent can germinate, and the seed is usually scattered within a yard or two of the parent. Moreover it takes three years from germination to sexual maturity. So by seed the dispersal rate averaged over a long period can only be about one foot per year.

On the whole, therefore, dog's mercury depends on its creeping rootstore for survival. Its natural habitat is a humus subsoil in shady woods and hedgerows; it does not like a sandy district, or a leached soil, which might cause it to disappear. It is thought that under ideal conditions dog's mercury will spread by vegetative means out of natural woodland at a rate of about nine or twelve inches a year, but six inches is more usual. On the evidence of the Monks Wood hedge there has been no lateral movement along the hedgerow from A into B or from E into D in the past 150 years.

Now, Dr Pollard's evidence is only from Huntingdonshire and it is important to see whether it holds elsewhere and to try to estimate a possible rate of spread into and along recent hedges radiating from old woodland. An example is Short Wood in Northamptonshire (Fig. 7). Short Wood lies about 200 feet above OD on the parish boundary between Southwick and Glapthorn. On the southern (Glapthorn) side are old enclosures with hedges known to be present in 1635. In these hedges dog's mercury has penetrated an average of 100 yards. On the northern (Southwick) side the hedges are recent and the dog's mercury has grown twenty yards along them. The rate of spread seems to be about nine inches a year. The two hedges to the west seem to contradict this but

---

* The perennial form of dog's mercury should not be confused with annual mercury, a weed of towns and gardens. This latter depends on fertilisation of its fruits for reproduction and does not have a creeping rootstock. It flowers in May or later, and is paler and less hairy than true dog's mercury.

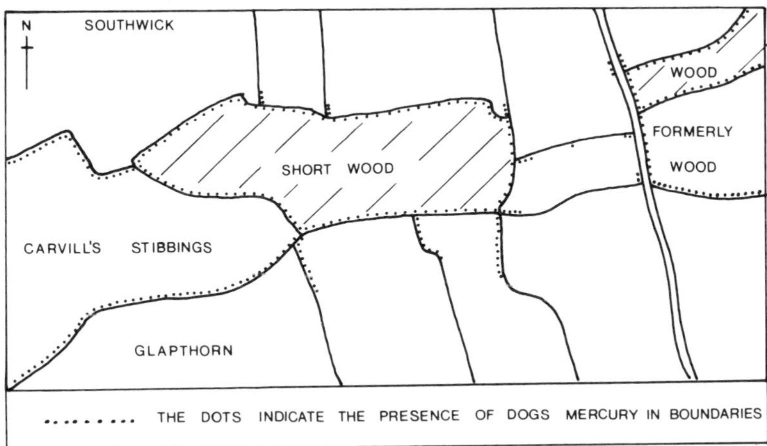

Fig. 7 Short wood (dog's mercury in boundaries)

as they are the boundaries of a close called Carvills Stibbings in 1635 and therefore probably assart hedges, they ought to have dog's mercury in them. A hedge on the east also seems odd but again it is an assart hedge since the field on the north side was a wood until a few years ago. So Pollard's postulate seems to work in Northamptonshire too.

The distribution of dog's mercury in Warwickshire indicates that it might also be true here, but whether the postulate would hold away from the clay soils of the midlands has yet to be determined. Even if it is true the question of its utility may also be raised. To this I must answer, regretfully and in an oblique manner, that I have yet to find an historian who considers counts of shrubs in hedgerows as real evidence. But it is my hope that this article may encourage some more people to look at hedges in a new light, for it is my belief that although ecologists can gain much from historical evidence historians will gain even more from ecological evidence.

Notes

1 O. Rackham, 'The history and effects of coppicing as a woodland practice', *Monks Wood Symposium* No. 3 (1967) pp. 82–93.
2 C. R. Tubbs, *The New Forest: an ecological history* (1968); G. F. Peterken, 'Development of vegetation in Staverton Park, Suffolk', *Field Studies* 3 (1969) pp. 1–39.
3 T. C. E. Wells, 'Land use changes affecting *pulsatilla vulgaris* in England', *Biol. Conservation* 1 (1968) pp. 37–43.
4 J. Sheail and T. C. E. Wells (eds), 'Old Grassland—its archaeological and ecological importance', *Monks Wood Symposium* No. 5 (1970).
5 M. D. Hooper, 'Dating hedges', *Area* 4 (1970) pp. 63–5.
6 E. Pollard, 'Hedges VII: woodland relic hedges in Huntingdon and Peterborough', *Journal of Ecology* (1973) (in press).

Urban surveys: medieval Oxford

This study of recent work in Oxford demonstrates something of both the value and limitations of the joint use of documentary and archaeological evidence. Its author, T. G. Hassall, *is Director of Excavations for the Oxford Archaeological Excavation Committee. His paper shows clearly that the documents provide the framework within which the archaeological evidence may be interpreted, even though on matters of detail there may be apparently irreconcilable differences between the two sources, and that for earlier periods, although archaeology may provide the bulk of the evidence, other sources may not be totally ignored.*

The field of urban studies is currently increasing at such a rapid pace that it would be impossible to give a wide-ranging view of all the work in progress within the scope of this short paper. The range of the work, both nationally and internationally, is amply demonstrated in the Digest section of the *Urban History Newsletter* Nos 1–13 (1963–9). It is thus proposed in this paper to look at the interrelationship between townscapes and documents in one town, Oxford, since experiences here have brought out into the open many of the problems likely to be encountered either by the solitary researcher or by a working group of adult students.[1]

Oxford: historical background

The late Saxon and medieval town of Oxford stands at the extreme tip of a gravel terrace.[2] In common with the other gravel terraces in the Upper Thames the site attracted early settlement. Neolithic and Bronze Age finds have been made, and where modern standing buildings and roads do not cover the ground aerial photography has brought to light prehistoric crop marks. The gravel soils cannot have supported a heavy woodland; the vegetation was therefore easily cleared, and once cleared it could be ploughed with light ploughs. The ground was well drained, although water was always near at hand. Few Iron Age finds have been discovered, but there is ample evidence for extensive Romano-British rural settlement. A minor Roman road, possibly utilising a pre-Roman route, is thought to have crossed the river at a ford at North Hinksey and then to have continued near the line of the present Oxford-Banbury road. The main centre of the Romano-British settlement was in the area of the modern suburbs of Headington, Cowley and Littlemore. Here there was a flourishing pottery industry whose wares were exported throughout southern Britain in the late third and fourth centuries. The pottery kilns were grouped along the main Roman road which ran from Alchester, on Akeman Street, through the little town of Dorchester-on-Thames to Silchester.

Virtually nothing is known about the site of Oxford in pagan Saxon times. At the time of the Conversion (*c.* 635) Dorchester-on-Thames, although hardly still urban, was clearly a royal centre and for a while it was the site of the first West Saxon bishopric. Oxford at this time was probably a part of the royal manor of Headington, where there was a royal villa. According to later tradition it was about 730 that a community of nuns and canons was established by St Frideswide on the site of the present Christ Church Cathedral. Elsewhere in the Thames valley the establishment of religious communities gave rise to small towns or trading centres. Oxford seems to have been no exception, and it was probably given a stimulus not only because of its position at what may have been the highest point of navigation on the river, but also because it was situated at the point where the main route between Mercia and Wessex crossed the river. This road from Northampton to Southampton was a major artery of Saxon and medieval England and in the Oxford region it replaced the Roman north-south route in importance.

In the early tenth century at the time of West Saxon *burh* building, it was Oxford and not Dorchester which was chosen as the regional administrative and military centre. In 912 Oxford is first mentioned in the *Anglo-Saxon Chronicle* and from that date the urban development of the town becomes clear. In Domesday it was the leading Midland town and it probably maintained its importance into the thirteenth century. The emergence of the university at the end of the twelfth century can have had little effect on the town's development at first, but by the early fourteenth century when Oxford's economic fortunes had begun to decline the university began to extend its influence over most aspects of the town's life. For a while the many religious communities in the town may have acted as something of a counter-weight, but after the Reformation the university's influence on the town was supreme.

During the seventeenth century the town began to expand again so that in size at least it was probably back to its thirteenth-century level.[3] However, there was little expansion in the eighteenth century. In the early nineteenth century two large working class suburbs, St Ebbe's and Jericho, were built and the end of the century witnessed extensive middle-class suburban development in north Oxford, once the fellows of colleges were allowed to marry. However, there were few sources of employment other than the university, the University Press, the Corporation and the railway companies. This situation was only changed with the establishment of large-scale industry, principally associated with motor-car production in east Oxford. Between the wars the town grew dramatically so that today Oxford is both a university city and a major industrial town.

Oxford's antiquarians

Oxford is extremely fortunate in that a great deal of evidence for the study of its past has survived. Furthermore the city has a long tradition of local historians and archaeologists who have made good use of the available documentary, topographical and archaeological sources. The presence of a resident academic population has been an important factor in the town's tradition of local studies. The first detailed topographical studies date from the seventeenth century, although there are earlier descriptions of the town like that of William Worcestre's of 1480. Leonard Hutten's (d. 1632) *Dissertation on the Antiquities of Oxford*, which was written about 1625–30, was the first attempt at a detailed description of the town and it makes a useful complement to the first map of Oxford, that of Ralph Agas (1578–88).[4] Contemporary with Hutten was Brian Twyne (*c*. 1579–1644) who from 1634 was the first Keeper of the University Archives. Most of Twyne's time seems to have been spent transcribing the wealth of manuscript material which survived in the university, city, ecclesiastical and college archives; Twyne's researches also took him to the public records and to the episcopal and chapter archives of Canterbury, Lincoln and Durham. Little of this material was ever published and it remained in manuscript amongst the university archives. The first person to make extensive use of Twyne's material was Anthony Wood (1632–95) who planned an elaborate study of Oxford based largely on Twyne whose work he hardly acknowledged. Wood's work was not published until 1773 when a badly edited version was printed under the title of *The Ancient and Present State of the City of Oxford*. It was not until Andrew Clark's edition of the *Survey of the Antiquities of the City of Oxford* that there was a definitive text generally available.[5]

In 1884 the Oxford Historical Society began the publication of primary sources for the city's history, and since that time the Society's publications have acted as a catalyst for documentary and topographical studies. As far as 'town', as opposed to 'gown', history is concerned, the most important names are probably those of James Parker, author of *The*

Early History of Oxford (727–1100), Andrew Clark, the editor of *Wood's History of the City of Oxford*, Herbert Hurst, author of *Oxford Topography*, and above all Herbert Edward Salter who edited no less than thirty-six volumes for the Society.[6] Salter's greatest topographical study was his unfinished *Survey of Oxford*, published after his death. In the *Survey* Salter attempted to reconstruct the topography of the medieval town from documentary sources.[7] He used as his base the first edition Ordnance Survey of 1878 whose details could be checked against a detailed rating survey of 1772. The hundred years between these two dates had witnessed massive changes in the topography of the town, but earlier than 1772 Salter demonstrated the static nature of the town's streets and property boundaries. By using charters and leases Salter was able to reconstruct the exact shape of medieval Oxford back to 1279 when the Hundred Rolls give the first full description of the town.

While Oxford has been fortunate in its documentary historians it has been equally fortunate in the calibre of researchers into the city's physical remains. It is hardly surprising that a town with such a wealth of architecture has attracted the attention of generations of draughtsmen. Naturally most artists have concentrated on university subjects, but some like Joseph Skelton or J. C. Buckler paid due attention to purely urban features. The buildings of Oxford have not only been drawn, they have also been surveyed and measured. By far the most detailed work is contained in the inventory of the Royal Commission on Historical Monuments, although this naturally concentrates on university buildings.[8] The work of Dr W. A. Pantin on vernacular domestic architecture has, however, redressed the imbalance and furthermore it has established a recording technique which has now been successfully employed elsewhere.[9]

Oxford also has a long history of archaeological research. The first excavation noted by the author was in 1583.[10] In that year the Corporation carried out a 'research excavation' in order to determine the exact line of the city wall during an ownership dispute between themselves and Merton College. The outcome of this excavation is not recorded. It was not however until 1876 that the first modern excavation took place. The area involved was that of the new Examination Schools in the High Street. The finds and contemporary accounts indicate that it was a typical domestic site of the late Saxon and medieval period, although the excavators were under the impression that the honeycomb of cess pits found were a 'British village'. In 1899 an important excavation on the city wall was conducted by the Oxford Architectural and Historical Society which successfully resolved a problem relating to the alignment of the wall.[11] In 1937 work on the new Bodleian Library brought about the first major 'rescue excavation' of recent times.[12] From this site R. L. S. Bruce-Mitford was able to establish the broad outlines of the local medieval pottery sequence and he thus inaugurated the period of scientific archaeo-

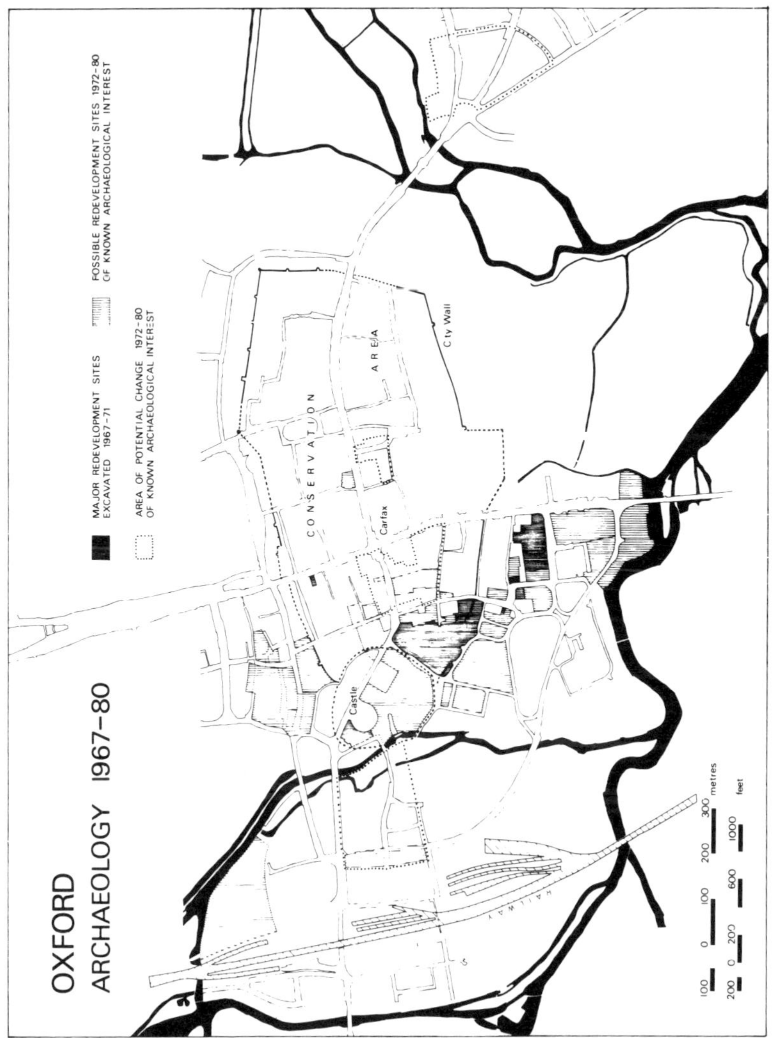

Fig. 8 Major redevelopment sites (Oxford)

logical research in the city which is principally associated with the name of Professor E. M. Jope. Jope's rescue and research excavations of the 1940s and 1950s demonstrated the vast potential of archaeology in discovering urban origins and topography in basically pre-documentary periods.[13] But in addition sites like the Clarendon Hotel in 1954–5 showed how the skilful use of archaeology, architecture and documentary history can be blended to produce something approaching a total urban survey.[14]

Oxford: modern excavations

The present archaeological survey in Oxford has been brought about by the massive redevelopment programme now taking place in the city (see Fig. 8). Oxford, like so many other historic towns, has been forced by a combination of economic circumstances and the motor car to rebuild much of its commercial district, notably in the western third of the late Saxon and medieval town. In this way nearly all of the city's accessible archaeology, ie areas outside the central conservation area where the historic fabric of the town is likely to remain largely intact, will be virtually destroyed during the next decade. The destruction will be brought about not only by modern building methods, but also by the very rigid high buildings' policy in Oxford which forces developers to build down rather than up in order to make a new building economically viable and at the same time preserve the city's famous skyline.

In 1966 the Field Department of the Oxford City and County Museum produced a survey entitled *City of Oxford Redevelopment: Archaeological Implications*. This report, now recognised as a model which has been repeated elsewhere, sought to identify and bring to the attention of planners and developers the immense destruction of the archaeological archive which was imminent. The report also led to a local awareness of the inadequacies of the then existing bodies to record below-ground material both before and during the construction of the new roads and buildings. Accordingly, in 1967 the Oxford Archaeological Excavation Committee was established to finance, co-ordinate and publish the results of a series of rescue and salvage excavations.

The actual excavations have largely been concentrated in what was historically the south-west ward. This ward contained a typical cross-section of urban and suburban sites. During the medieval period the ward would have been dominated by two large friaries; the Greyfriars and the Blackfriars. The Reformation created a vacuum in the area which was perhaps surprisingly not filled by the university, and the sites of these religious houses were not built over until the second quarter of the nineteenth century when a large working-class suburb was developed, known as St Ebbe's.[15] It is this suburb and the immediately adjoining areas of the medieval town which are currently the subject of urban renewal. Although there are some new houses, St Ebbe's has virtually ceased to be a residential area and henceforward it is likely to be dominated by multi-storey car-parks and a large shopping centre, the Westgate, together with associated commercial development.

The two sources

The archaeological work that was carried out on the Westgate site from 1968–72 demonstrates fairly clearly what archaeology, combined with documentary research, has to offer the urban historian. Before excavations began, the documentary work of H. E. Salter provided a good outline of the potential of the area (see Fig. 9). Although to the untutored eye there was little of historical interest above ground, the topography of the site, including streets, many property boundaries and the line of the city wall, had remained virtually unchanged since the thirteenth century. With the exception of the line of the city wall the new development has taken no account of this topographical legacy. The destruction of the topography above ground and the archaeology below ground is now practically total.

In spite of Salter's work it seemed desirable to ensure that the documentary survey was complete, particularly in view of the acquisition and central storage by the Corporation of a vast additional archive of property deeds as a result of compulsory purchase orders. The work of up-dating the documentary survey was carried out by Dr Hilary Turner who has established the complete tenurial structure of the Westgate site as far as the documents will allow. Dr Turner's work has emphasised the completeness of Salter's survey for this area of the town at least, but at the same time it has been particularly valuable in demonstrating the dismemberment of the Greyfriars' site and the growth of courts and rows in the nineteenth century. This documentary research was of enormous value in establishing excavation priorities. But the documents are so much concerned with legal and tenurial matters that they can provide only a skeletal framework. The archaeological aspect has added the flesh and blood.

The actual excavations conducted on the Westgate site had to be phased with the programme of demolition and construction (see Fig. 10). In this respect they reflected one of the major drawbacks of all rescue excavation, namely that it is the developer who dictates which sites become available for excavation rather than the archaeologist. In this situation it is very important for the archaeologist to be clear in his own mind what his excavation priorities are, but it is still possible to carry through a research programme within a rescue framework. If the archaeologist in Oxford had been free to select a large site to excavate in the centre of the City, the Westgate site is not necessarily the one that he would have chosen. St Ebbe's is not older than anywhere else in the city although the church is the first in the city to be documented, being mentioned in 1005. However, the site had one very real advantage.

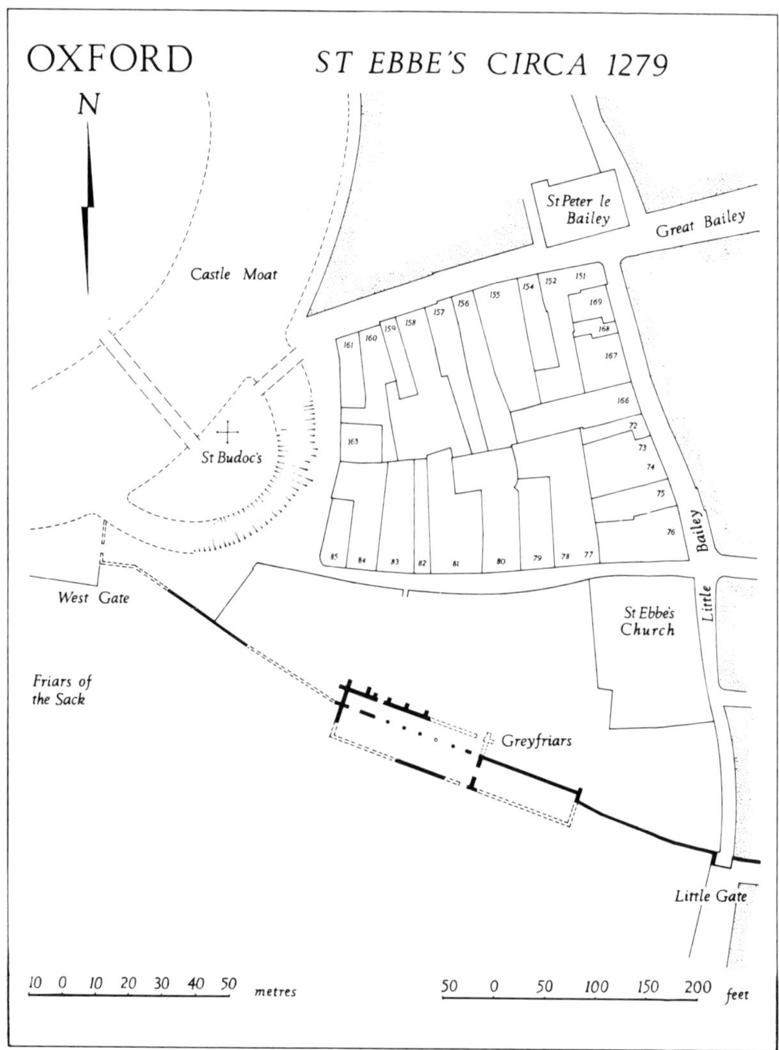

Fig. 9 St Ebbe's, *circa* 1279

Extending as it does from the city wall to the centre of the town, it is rather like a wedge-shaped slice in the archaeological layer cake at Oxford. Within this slice was a whole range of sites reflecting practically every aspect of late Saxon and medieval town life including ordinary domestic houses, the city wall, the very important Franciscan friary, two late Saxon and medieval streets, a little parish church (the church of St Budoc, destroyed 1215–16) and an outer defence of Oxford castle.

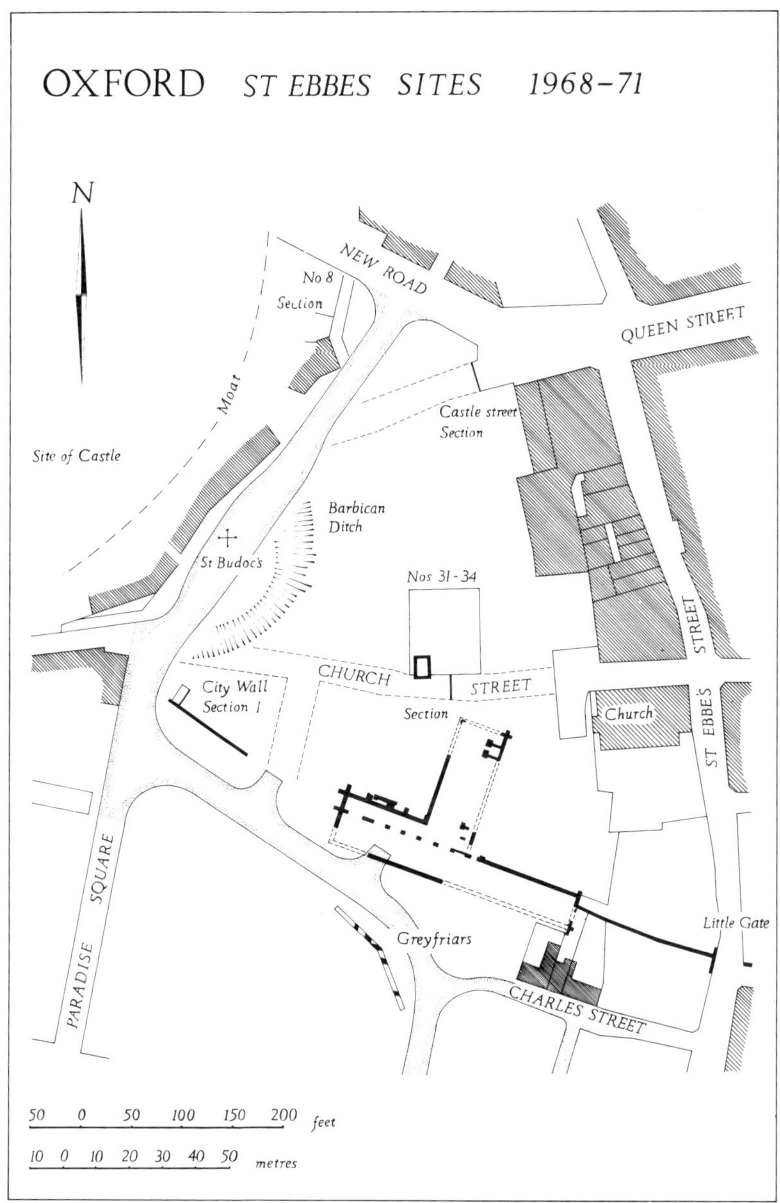

Fig. 10 St Ebbe's sites 1968–71

The development was on so large a scale that in some places there was ample time to excavate well in advance of building while adjoining properties were acquired and demolished and streets and services were re-routed. Certain specific parts were chosen for prior excavation where this was feasible. These included areas of domestic occupation on the north side of Church Street and the city wall, both to the west and east of the Greyfriars, as well as the Greyfriars church. The general position of these features was known from documentary research carried out before excavations began. A second phase of the archaeological work involved keeping a constant watch on the whole site while the new service basement was being carved out. At this stage a small team of archaeologists was constantly at work excavating areas as they were uncovered by bulldozers. Sites excavated at this time included Castle Street and Church Street and the castle barbican; salvaging of domestic material throughout the whole site was also carried out.

The first excavations were concentrated on the major domestic site in Church Street, since archaeology can provide extensive information on social and economic history which the documents simply do not cover.[16] The documents indicated that from the thirteenth century at least there were two properties on the site. The eastern two-thirds of the area eventually excavated was owned by Lincoln College and called during the middle ages, *Domus Mirifeld*. The college divided it up into separate tenements and eventually there were three houses on the site. The remaining western third of the excavated area was one single property, which for a short while in the fourteenth century was an academic hall, known as Whitehall. Such a hall would have accommodated students, for the bulk of the student population of the medieval university was housed in private and licensed lodging houses of this sort rather than in colleges.

In spite of very limited modern disturbance on the street frontage, little remained of the medieval timber structures. The plans of two buildings only could be reconstructed, the one on the *Domus Mirifeld* site was sub-rectangular, constructed in the thirteenth century of upright wooden posts; the other, a rectangular building of the fourteenth century on the Whitehall site, consisted of a dry stone footing for supporting the ground beams.

This lack of structural remains is usual in Oxford where the medieval houses were almost invariably of timber construction which leaves little or no trace in the ground, unless the timbers were placed on dry stone wall footings. Furthermore the street frontages are usually extensively disturbed by more recent cellars except in the city's low-lying south suburb, St Aldate's. Indeed the most complete series of house foundations have been recently recovered at Nos. 79–80 St Aldate's. No. 79 St Aldate's, which stood at the corner of a side street, Speedwell Street, was particularly interesting. It afforded one of the rare instances of a direct correlation between documentary and archaeological evidence. In 1439

Oseney Abbey leased a tenement for four shillings to Nicholas Fairway and his wife Joan.[17] The lease gives a full description of the building which is described as a shop with a 'solar' (living room) above. Its measurements and given as 10 feet and 1 inch along the high road (St Aldate's) and 16 feet 2 inches along the lane (Overee's Lane). These dimensions are very close to those of the footings of the building as excavated.

Although the Church Street tenements provided little information on structure, the internal divisions and uses of the site were typical. Behind the houses were courtyards, sometimes spread with gravel surfaces, and containing wells which were the only means of supplying water to the occupants. The gardens behind the courtyards were essential for the disposal of domestic rubbish. The pits in which the refuse was buried contains the bulk of the material available to the archaeologist when attempting to reconstruct social and economic conditions. Naturally the view of life which emerges from this evidence is rather biased because such material has all been deliberately discarded. In addition, many objects will not survive the passage of time unless the condition of the soil in which they are buried is suitable. However, in spite of these limitations much can be learnt from such apparently unpromising material.

The development in St Ebbe's gave a very valuable opportunity to study the city wall, which the documentary evidence suggested had to be modified in this part of the town due to problems arising from the building of the Greyfriars. From 1226 onwards Henry III was encouraging Oxford, through murage grants, to expend money on the repair and rebuilding of the wall. In St Ebbe's the wall extended from a small postern called the Watergate or, more commonly, the Little Gate to the West Gate, near the castle.

When the Greyfriars came to St Ebbe's in 1224 they began to acquire properties on both sides of the wall between the two gates.[18] By about 1244 they owned or controlled all the land from Church Street down to the nearest branch of the Thames, the Trill Mill Stream. Once the friars had acquired this land they naturally wanted to extend their buildings. However, the only suitable place for building was directly in the line between the West Gate and Little Gate. Here the ground was reasonably level and at the same time was not too marshy, but in order to build the friars had to obtain royal consent because it was crossed both by the wall and a street described as 'under' the wall.

In 1244 Henry III allowed the friars to enclose the street, probably a continuation of Brewer Street, and to take down the wall where it was in the way of the new church. However, Henry's grant was conditional. In return the friars had to build a new wall from the western side of the Little Gate southwards to the Trill Mill Stream and along its banks to a point where it could turn northwards again to rejoin the old wall at the West Gate. Such a construction would have been quite beyond the means of the Greyfriars, who were also heavily engaged in building their new church. Accordingly in 1248 the king issued another grant allowing the friars to enclose the street and take down the wall, with the north side of the church supplying the interruption. The wall at either end was simply to be repaired. This complicated sequence was revealed in the excavations which uncovered the western side of the Little Gate, the partially built wall of 1244 running south towards the Thames, and the wall both east and west of the church lying astride it.

Until the recent excavations it was very difficult to gather information on the Greyfriars church. No trace survived above ground, and the only definite information about it was a description made in 1480 by William Worcestre, England's first architectural historian.[19] Between 1478 and 1480 Worcestre travelled across southern England describing buildings of interest on his journeys. The descriptions in his notebooks are often very detailed and include dimensions of buildings. Unfortunately William Worcestre did not carry a tape measure with him, and his measurements are not always accurate. Obviously, attempting to reconstruct a now vanished building from these somewhat unreliable figures is rather fruitless. An added complication in the case of the Oxford Greyfriars was that it had a plan unusual for an English friary church, for it included an extension, a hundred feet long, like a transept in its northern side, so that the fully developed plan was like an inverted 'T'.

In the foregoing sites the complementary nature of the sources has been emphasised, but a further site in St Ebbe's excavated during the salvage phase will serve to show how, in largely pre-documentary periods, the archaeological evidence may be the only kind available. A complete section was obtained through Queen Street, which forms part of the main east-west axis of the town. Altogether there were eighteen road surfaces, including the modern one. The lowest seven had been cut through by rubbish pits of the late Saxon period, while the first surface had pottery resting on it which can provisionally be dated to the early tenth century. This street section provided a dramatic example of how important archaeology is becoming in discovering the origins of a town like Oxford. Subsequent excavations on the site in St Aldate's, alluded to above, have now extended the archaeological sequence in the town back to the late eighth century, long before the first reference to the town in the *Anglo-Saxon Chronicle* in 912.

The destruction of the St Ebbe's sites is virtually complete and the work of synthesis has begun. It is hoped to bring together all the available evidence, documentary, topographical and archaeological, in order to present a picture of the development of this typical urban area. It should, for instance, be possible to produce maps from the late thirteenth century onwards at approximately one-hundred-year intervals which will summarise the information. This study should provide a microcosm of late Saxon, medieval and post-medieval Oxford which will not only be of value for this town, but also for other English, and indeed continental, towns.

Urban investigation

The excavations in St Ebbe's, Oxford, demonstrate one typical urban survey area. The chief lesson learnt was that in order to recover the total history of a town, archives and archaeology have an equal and complementary role to play. The relative importance of the archaeological aspect increases in pre-documentary periods. The chief distinguishing characteristic of the two sources of evidence appears to be that while documents are increasingly well-cared for, the archaeological material is diminishing at an alarming rate. By the end of the century only the smallest historic towns will have any accessible urban archaeology remaining.[20]

Meanwhile, in places like Oxford where resources exist, something is being done to salvage the material record of the past. In addition, other aspects of urban survey work are being carried out by other bodies. For instance the Victoria County History is active in the town, and the section on Oxford for the *Historic Towns Atlas* is in preparation, as well as the History of the University. These are all highly professional projects, but even here there is scope for participation by the extra-mural student. In the case of the excavations this participation is at varying levels. Regular classes are held to explain the progress of the excavations, and the Excavation Committee runs joint weekend courses with the Oxford University Department for External Studies on topics such as late Saxon town defences. Adult students also take an active part including digging, processing the finds, pottery drawing and the compilation of a sites and monuments record. One class is involved in a study of the 1851 census of St Ebbe's. Amateur involvement has always been one of the strengths of British archaeology and extra-mural departments can make a major contribution towards solving the current crisis facing urban archaeology.

Notes

1 Many of the general points raised in this article are dealt with in greater detail by Martin Biddle in Archaeology and the History of British Towns, *Antiquity* XLII (1968) pp. 109–16 and also in Historical Research, the report of the C.B.A. study group, *Conservation and Development*, ed. Pamela Ward (1968) pp. 127–55. Archaeological research in towns other than Oxford is conveniently summarised in the conference papers of the C.B.A. Conference, Urban History: Archaeological Research in Progress, held at Nottingham University in 1971.

2 For late Saxon and medieval Oxford see E. M. Jope, Saxon Oxford and its Region, *Dark Age Britain,* ed. D. B. Harden (1956) pp. 234–58; H. E. Salter, *Medieval Oxford*, Oxford Historical Society C (1936).
3 For a later history of Oxford see Ruth Fasnacht *A History of the City of Oxford* (1954) chaps X–XIX.
4 H. Hurst, *Oxford Topography*, Oxford Historical Society XXXIX (1899).
5 *Wood's City of Oxford,* ed. A. Clark, Vols I–III, Oxford Historical Society XV (1889), XVII (1890), XXXVII (1899).
6 J. Parker, *The Early History of Oxford 727–1100*, Oxford Historical Society III (1884–1885); H. Hurst, *Oxford Topography.*
7 H. E. Salter, *Survey of Oxford*, Vols I and II, ed. W. A. Pantin, Oxford Historical Society, New series XIV (1960), XX (1969).
8 R.C.H.M., *Oxford* (1939).
9 W. A. Pantin, Development of Domestic Architecture in Oxford, *Antiquaries Journal*, XXVII (1947) pp. 120–50.
10 W. H. Turner, *Records of the City of Oxford* (1880), p. 433.
11 F. H. Penny, *Buried Oxford Unearthed* (1899).
12 R. L. S. Bruce-Mitford, 'The archaeology of the site of the Bodleian extension in Broad Street, Oxford', *Oxoniensia* IV (1939) pp. 89–146.
13 E. M. Jope, 'Saxon Oxford and its region', in *Dark Age Britain*, ed. D. B. Harden (1956) pp. 234–58.
14 E. M. Jope and W. A. Pantin, 'The Clarendon Hotel, Oxford, parts I and II', *Oxoniensia* XXIII (1958) pp. 1–129.
15 This process is discussed by R. J. Morris in 'The friars and paradise: an essay in the building history of Oxford, 1801–1861', *Oxoniensia* XXXVI (1971) pp. 72–98.
16 All the following excavations are discussed in more detail in the interim reports of the excavations in Oxford published in *Oxoniensia* XXXIV–XXXVII. A popular account of all the recent excavations in Oxford is contained in T. G. Hassall, *Oxford, the City beneath your feet* (1972).
17 Salter, *Survey of Oxford* p. 22.
18 A. G. Little, *The Grey Friars in Oxford*. Oxford Historical Society XX (1891) chap. II.
19 J. H. Harvey, *William Worcestre Itineraries* (1969) pp. ix–xvii, 273.
20 *The Erosion of History*, ed. C. M. Heighway (1972).

Later urban landscapes

The integration of urban landscapes and documents has in recent years been most successfully exploited in the study of nineteenth-century towns; but as Vanessa Doe, *Staff Tutor in the Department of Extra-Mural Studies, University of Sheffield, points out here, even in nineteenth-century studies there is more to be done, and the same principles apply to towns in the early modern period. Her paper is based on work done on Bradford, Halifax and King's Lynn.*

Although it is becoming unusual now to pick up a recent publication on urban history and find in it no references at all to the visible evidence of urban development, there is still a good deal of uncertainty about how such evidence can be used. In the main, illustrations still tend to be collected for antiquarian purposes. They record the appearance of a street, a building or a monument, but they are not used to further our understanding of it in its proper historical context. For instance, the recent spate of illustrated guides to the historic architecture of northern industrial cities are almost purely antiquarian in outlook.[1] They have provided us with a splendid photographic record of many streets and buildings, but if there is any recognisable order at all it is at best in terms of architectural history and at worst simply chronological. Much of the topographical and architectural record still has to be interpreted and the economic, social and political context explored to further our understanding of the contemporary urban environment.

Nineteenth-century urban growth: Bradford

The use of manuscript sources in conjunction with the physical evidence to explain the nature of urban development is particularly rewarding in nineteenth-century towns where a very great deal of both types of evidence survives. The uses of documents and buildings in the field of industrial archaeology have been examined elsewhere in this volume.[2] Much valuable work has already been done using a combination of sources on nineteenth-century housing. The work of Professor Beresford in Leeds, Dr Stanley Chapman in Nottingham, Dr Jennifer Tann in Birmingham[3] and others is beginning to reveal the success of an approach to documents and landscapes which must surely bear fruit in other fields as well. Much in the way of nineteenth-century housing still survives to be photographed, measured and mapped. The type of development can then be analysed, its layout related to the pattern of land ownership, to the scale of land values, to the pressure of building bye-laws and other determining factors, through the study of relevant documents —deeds and estate papers, newspaper advertisements, local bye-laws and the applications to build submitted to the local authorities. By using both types of sources, for example, Professor Beresford has succeeded in explaining the reason for early back-to-back housing developments in Leeds.[4] The debate on housing standards can also be taken a step further when the documentary evidence of overcrowding taken from the census or such indirect sources as local Board of Health inquiries can be related to room sizes, sanitary facilities and local amenities like parks and other open spaces.

Industry and housing provide the most obvious areas of study but commercial activity in nineteenth-century towns similarly gave rise to vast rebuilding programmes. In this field also much remains to be seen on the ground, and the actual process of development is documented in a number of sources. Copies of Improvement Acts to enable a Corporation to rebuild roads in central areas generally survive, accompanied by maps showing the original line of streets and buildings. The clearing away and rebuilding is usually reported in great detail in the local press, and the prestige offices and shops, whether by local or nationally famous architects, are frequently discussed in trade and professional periodicals like the *Builder*. The study of this process is particularly worthwhile because it so often reveals just how Victorians saw their cities, and how they articulated the problems of architectural design in the light of social and commercial ideals.

Victorian Bradford, for example, was the result of an almost total redevelopment of the central area of the old city over a single decade between 1870 and 1880. Practically nothing now remains of pre-industrial Bradford, at least in the town centre. This astonishing phenomenon was reported by the inevitable 'Bystander' in the *Bradford Observer*:[5]

> 'Then it was that old Bradford crumbled swiftly away and new Bradford sprang into existence as if by Magic. People who had been absent from the town for ten years did not know it again when they returned

to it. All was changed. Palatial warehouses, magnificent shops, imposing churches, large hotels, splendid public buildings, beautiful mansions and new streets without end arose out of the ruins, and Bradford with its new face of stone was something for the artistic mind to admire.'

'Bystander' in another article significantly refers to the 'Italian' quality of the town's architecture, and to the view down Market Street which to him was the very reincarnation of Florence as he believed it to have been in the heyday of the Renaissance. The winning design for the new Town Hall in 1869 incorporated a replica of the campanile from Florence's Palazzo Pubblico, and had the by then distinctly fashionable gothic informality of design (see Figs. 11a and 11b). Lockwood and Mayson, the local firm of architects who with another firm, Andrews and Pepper, must claim responsibility for practically the entire town centre redevelopment, were adept at achieving monumentality with an architectural vocabulary derived from mainly Italian sources, both gothic and classical. And it suited Bradford. It carried the appropriate overtones of commercial success.[6]

The history of street development in Bradford town centre can be traced in the maps attached to the 1873 Improvement Act. The plans for the buildings were submitted for approval by the borough engineer and still survive. Architects can almost always be traced from this source, although such an important phase in the building history of Bradford received almost weekly attention in the *Builder* from about 1868. The cost of many projects is mentioned there. And of course there is the local press comment.

Other aspects of nineteenth-century urban development can be explored in this way. Parks for example often reveal in their design and layout not so much how working people actually took their recreation, but how the factory masters who promoted and financed the construction of these open spaces hoped they would. The People's Park in Halifax was laid out by Paxton in 1856–7 and financed by Francis Crossley, a local and very wealthy carpet manufacturer.[7] It was 'an arrangement of art and nature' to bring beauty within walking distance of the homes of Halifax working men, an opportunity for a man to 'take his stroll there after he has done his hard day's toil', no doubt to think or converse about morally uplifting subjects. Active recreation was expressly forbidden—no cricket, bowls or hockey, and no music on Sundays; such activities may perhaps have been expected to encourage self-assertion, and to undermine the meek acceptance of daily work. On the other hand theatres, music halls and pubs still survive to bring alive other aspects of recreational facilities in nineteenth-century towns.

Fig. 11a Bradford Town Hall.

Bradford Public Library Illustration Collection

Fig. 11 Italian townscape in nineteenth-century Bradford. (*a*) Bradford Town Hall, opened in 1873. The architects were the local firm of Lockwood and Mawson, but they clearly owed much to Burges' competition design for the London Law Courts. (*b*) The Wool Exchange, Market Street. This too was designed by the versatile Lockwood and Mawson. Palmerstone laid the foundation stone in 1864 and the building was opened in 1867. Both buildings are still standing.

Fig. 11b Bradford Wool Exchange

Early modern towns: King's Lynn

To anyone working on nineteenth-century towns the enormous gains of taking documentary and physical evidence together must be obvious. But such techniques can also be used to explore earlier phases of urban development. The volume of material may not be anything like as great, and it may be much more uneven in quality. A town with good official records, prosperous and expanding up to the sixteenth and seventeenth centuries, but in which subsequently the rate of growth was considerably cut back, is an obvious choice for anyone wishing to study the earlier stages of pre-industrial urban society. One such town is King's Lynn.[8] Founded as a new town at the end of the eleventh century by the Bishop of Norwich, it achieved immediate and spectacular success as a port. Its sheltered harbour in the mouth of the Little Ouse was used by merchants from overseas, while its extensive hinterland to the south was well served by river transport. By the beginning of the thirteenth century its volume of trade was second only to that of Southampton among the provincial ports. King's Lynn remained a thriving port until the beginning of the eighteenth century, although by the fifteenth century it was declining in relation to other towns. This relative decline, however, is not reflected in the built environment of the town where the rate of rebuilding remained unaffected. Much more important was Lynn's ability to weather the problems of a changing pattern of trade and avoid the losses which caused serious decline in absolute terms in other east coast towns. Lynn remained buoyant until serious difficulties to shipping were caused by fen drainage schemes in the eighteenth century; and finally succumbed, as did other coastal towns, to competition from the railways in the mid-nineteenth century.

Lynn then was a town where there was sufficient wealth to ensure that the fabric of the town developed to keep pace with the changing pattern of commercial activity until the end of the seventeenth century but where, fortunately, major rebuilding in the eighteenth and nineteenth centuries was avoided. Thus the town is a neat fossil, and with the exception of a skin-deep veneer of twentieth-century commercialism is still much as it was in general scale and appearance in the days of its prosperity as a port. It is also fortunate in possessing an exceptionally good collection of written records. Thus not only is the fabric there to be inspected, but the records exist to enable the student to interpret with some confidence what he sees.

A glance at a map of Lynn (Fig. 12) will show that the town is divided into three parts by ancient watercourses. The Purfleet, the northernmost stream flowing through the built-up area, seems to separate two self-contained communities, each with its own church and market place. The southernmost sector, with the Millfleet as its northern boundary, appears as yet a third community, rather more sparsely populated, yet with its own church. An examination of the physical remains shows the differences and similarities between these areas in more detail. To the north of the Purfleet is an exceptionally large market place, the Tuesday Market formerly adjoining an open waterfront area on the west, known as the Common Staithe. St Nicholas Chapel is a large, predominantly fifteenth-century structure just outside the area of the market place to the north-east. The scale of development has clearly not altered greatly since the seventeenth century. The largest houses are those which line the sides of the Tuesday Market and spread along the streets leading from the market along the bank of the river, King Street running southwards and St Nicholas Street and St Ann's Street curving round to the north from its eastern corner. Most of these large houses have ranges of warehouses and other outbuildings attached. The streets to the east or landward side of the market are lined with on the whole much smaller houses occupying smaller plots and without the extensive ranges of outbuildings.

A similar pattern of development can be found in the area to the south between the Purfleet and the Millfleet. There, however, the market place is smaller and overshadowed by the large parish church of St Margaret on the one side and the medieval guildhall on the other. Again the larger houses occupy the areas which adjoined the market place or where there was immediate access to the river Ouse. Even a superficial examination will reveal that not only substantial parts of the houses but of the warehouses too are medieval and have not been much altered since the fifteenth century.

In contrast South Lynn, to the south of the Millfleet, has no immediately recognisable commercial centre, although it has a church, All Saints, of great antiquity, and several large houses which appear to date from the fifteenth to the seventeenth century. A perambulation will reveal that only a small part of this area was built on before the nineteenth century, mainly along the line of a street which led beside the river to the South Gate and the bridge over the river Nar. The nineteenth-century housing which now covers much of South Lynn shows no sign of having been planned around an already existing street pattern, and indeed we know that in the seventeenth century the considerable area of open ground in South Lynn was used for grazing, drying fish and for rope walks.

Even after the most superficial examination of the town important questions will have emerged, and although intelligent guesswork may provide some answers it is at this point that the documentary sources must be consulted. Some material is printed, and most towns will have at least one history written probably at the end of the nineteenth century in which the writer will have attempted to collect the available information on the origins of the settlement and has at least recorded any known dates of the prinicpal buildings. In Lynn such sources[9] reveal that when the bishop of Norwich founded the town in *c.* 1098

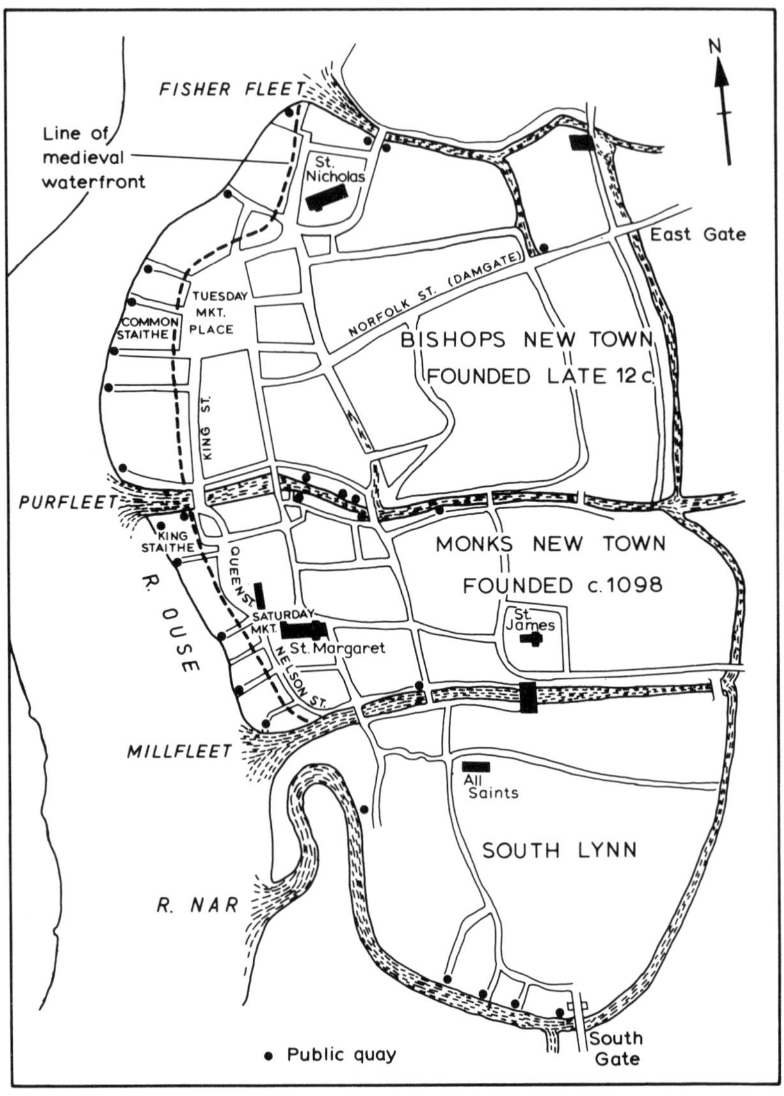

Fig. 12 South Lynn

he did so on the part of his manor of Gaywood next to the estuarine lake or 'lyn' bounded on the north by the Purfleet and on the south by the Millfleet. There he established a priory which he subsequently gave to the monks of Norwich Cathedral Priory along with 'land, marsh and people' and the grant of a 'sand market' on Saturdays. Subsequent bishops, finding the monks' town was a success, probably encouraged the development of a further settlement northward onto land which was still under their direct lordship in the latter half of the eleventh century. The two towns no doubt saw themselves as rivals, the bishops and the monks competing for revenues on adjoining sites. The northern township was granted its own market, held on Tuesdays, and a chapel was established which never in fact attained independent parochial status. Eventually the bishops made an exchange with the monks and re-assumed their control over the whole site to the north of the Millfleet, obtaining for it a charter in 1204 in the name of Bishops Lynn. South Lynn has always been the poor relation. The site was no better and no worse than that chosen by the bishop for his new town. It just happened to lie in another manor, the lord of which never seems to have taken the slightest interest in its commercial potential.

Lynn, then, was not one town but three during the most formative early period of urban growth, and they were all under different lordships. This explains the duplication of market places, the three principal churches and, bearing in mind the usual method of setting out the streets of a new town on a grid pattern, the general layout of the site. We need further evidence, however, to help us understand the type of development which took place in Lynn and the ways in which the different occupational groups in the town adapted themselves to maximise the potential of the site.

If one source can be singled out for this kind of investigation, it must be deeds and charters. These exist in considerable numbers for some towns and are of course especially helpful if, like the Oxford collection, there are sufficient runs on a number of adjacent sites to show in some detail what the pattern of land use was.[10] Few towns, however, can draw on such exhaustive collections. In Lynn there are several types of records particularly helpful in establishing who occupied a site and how he used his land—the sixteenth-century surveys made by the town chamberlain to ensure that the rents due to the corporation were collected, the chamberlains' rentals, and the council minute books, or Hall Books, which contain a vast amount of incidental information on property and building. Probate records are also helpful, although in Lynn most people of any substance obtained probate in the Prerogative Court of Canterbury, so that unfortunately the accompanying inventories have not until recently been available for inspection. Wills registered in Norwich however have been useful, and seventeenth and early eighteenth-century inventories are fairly plentiful for the lesser men of the town.

In Lynn there is a distinct pattern of zoning by occupation which is somewhat unusual in pre-industrial towns. It is this which causes the clear difference in the scale and quality of building between the waterfront areas in the town and those further inland. This seems to have been the result of the demand by merchants for waterfront sites. We know for example that in the town rentals in the early seventeenth century all of King Street and Queen Street, St Nicholas Street, St Ann's Street, Purfleet Street and most of Nelson Street and Stonegate Street were taken up with the property of men who appear in the Freemen's Register as merchants. These men were, inevitably in a community which depended entirely on trade, the most prosperous group in the town, office holders in the council and the owners of substantial farms in the surrounding country districts. Practically all of their goods came to the town in ships, coastwise or from overseas, and left in barges and lighters for destinations inland. Warehouse space and facilities for loading and unloading vessels on the waterfront were clearly of great importance to them, and they built their houses nearby. This juxtaposition of merchant's house and business premises is not of course at all unusual in a period when business was done by face-to-face dealings, and where supervision of the business was still carried out by the owner himself.

The concentration of merchant properties on the waterfront in Lynn raises two further questions, both of which can be answered by an examination of surviving seventeenth-century buildings alongside detailed study of contemporary sources. First, can the distribution of merchant property *outside* the obvious river bank area tell us anything about water communications elsewhere in the town? Secondly, what was the relative importance of the various waterfront areas; does the relationship change from one period to another?

The plotting of merchant property on a map, both where there are surviving buildings and from documentary references, indicates that the Purfleet and to a lesser extent the Millfleet were navigable for some distance into the town. The Nar on the other hand never seems to have attracted merchant shipping, and the Fisher Fleet, the outfall of the Gaywood River in the extreme north of the town, was similarly ignored. Unfortunately the whole of the Fisher Fleet area has been rebuilt, part in the nineteenth century when the new docks were laid out and the rest more recently for road improvement. It was however the core of Lynn's fishing community. In the seventeenth century fishermen made representations to the Privy Council to the effect that merchants mooring vessels in the Fleet were causing great inconvenience to fishing boats, and there are several references in the Hall Books to the leasing of property and anchorages to fishermen.

The success of the fishermen in excluding merchants from a safe and suitable harbour may be partly explained by examining the reasons which underlay preferences for certain parts of the waterfront on the part of merchants. One of the determining factors seems to have been the proximity of the market place. It is possible to note, for example, the changing location of the commercial centre of the town as market facilities in one area deteriorated while in another they improved. The Saturday Market was the hub of commercial activity in the medieval town. The guildhall of the foremost merchant guild, that of the Holy Trinity, was located in it, and evidence of substantial stone-built houses and warehouses of medieval origin have been found nearby. By the sixteenth century this market area was losing its attraction. The open space had become cluttered with semi-permanent and permanent shops, while there was no public landing stage of any size nearer than the King's Staithe at the top of Queen Street, and no public warehouses which could be leased by visiting merchants to store their wares. The town's merchants migrated from the area, and their old properties were brought up and renovated to become the town houses of the gentry from the surrounding countryside.

As the Saturday Market declined, so the Tuesday Market appears to have increased in importance. This market square was, and still is, one of the largest in England and, in the sixteenth and seventeenth centuries, was almost entirely free from encroachment. A great variety of goods could thus be dealt in there, and the market was divided into various sectors for the sale of different wares. Adjoining the market place was a large and well equipped quay, with twenty or so public warehouses. By 1600 many properties in the nearby waterfront streets had been rebuilt by the town's most wealthy merchants. A perambulation of the area would quickly show how prosperous it was, and so it remained until the end of the eighteenth century.

The location of the merchant premises was, then, determined by two factors—access to water transport and proximity to the open market place. It is the latter of these which helps to explain why the Fisher Fleet area was not sought after by merchants as much as one would have expected. It would have given access to the river, but was obviously too far distant from the Tuesday market place to make it a prime attraction.

The scope for the kind of investigation in which observation of the fabric of the town goes hand in hand with a search through the records for further information is almost inexhaustible in a place like Lynn, and can be used to examine aspects of the town's history at practically every level one might choose. By no means all urban historians will be so fortunate. Often the peeling off process, in which one is almost literally physically removing the accretions of subsequent rebuilding to the point in time chosen to mark the beginning of one's own investigation, will be so time-consuming and exhausting that little more than a record of the above-ground archaeology can be attempted. Some towns may well have fossilised in a period for which there is little or no useful documentary source material. In such circumstances greater reliance would have to be placed on the physical evidence, but much of value may be extracted from it once the techniques have been mastered. Again, some towns may be well documented but lack material remains. There will however always be something worth recording in the field—the street plan, street names, parish boundaries, a handful of old cottages. None of these should be neglected.

Without the use of both documents and physical remains the history of towns remains incomplete. This is true of towns in all stages of their development, and it is just as important to use both types of evidence in writing the history of towns as it is in writing the history of the rural landscape. The uneven survival of historical evidence will always be a problem, but unlikely places have often yielded rich rewards to the historian with an open mind and an ability to use a wide variety of approaches.

Notes

1 See, for example, Bruce Allsopp, *Historic Architecture of Newcastle-on-Tyne* (1968); Derek Linstrum, *Historic Architecture of Leeds* (1969); Dennis Sharp, *Manchester* (1969); Brian Little, *Birmingham Buildings* (1971); John Ayers, *Architecture in Bradford* (1972).

2 p. 75.

3 See S. D. Chapman (ed.), *The History of Working Class Housing* (1971); A. Rogers, *This Was Their World* (1972), pp. 59–63; M. W. Beresford and G. R. J. Jones, *Leeds and its Region* (1967), pp. 186–97. See also H. J. Dyos, *Victorian Suburb* (1961).

4 Chapman, pp. 96–104.

5 *Bradford Observer* 1883.

6 Ayers, *Bradford*, pp. 7–37.

7 W. Creese, *The Search for Environment* (1966), pp. 48–55.

8 Vanessa Parker, *The Making of King's Lynn* (1971).

9 Charles Parkin, 'Topography of Freebridge Hundred and Half in the County of Norfolk', in Blomefield's *Norfolk* VIII (1808); E. M. Beloe, *Our Borough* (1871); H. J. Hillen, *History of the Borough of King's Lynn* (1907).

10 See above, p. 51.

Industrial archaeology

In this paper Barrie Trinder, *tutor organiser for the County Council of Salop, argues persuasively for a full and integrated study of both the documentary and material evidence from the past in any study of industrial history; and that no landscape historian can afford to ignore industrial archaeology in his interpretation of what he can see around him.*

Defining industrial archaeology has lately become a popular pastime.[1] In a short study of this kind an excess of pontification over definitions seems unnecessary. We mean by the term the use of archaeological techniques and approaches, such as surveying, measuring, excavating, laboratory analysis and geographical fieldwork, in the investigation of industrial history. It is the theme of this paper that the study of existing remains can, in many cases, add a significant new dimension to our understanding of industrial history and that the potentialities of industrial archaeology have as yet hardly begun to be realised.

Industrial archaeology: the techniques

The term 'industrial archaeology' was first used in print by Michael Rix in 1955.[2] Rix drew particular attention to the educational and aesthetic aspects of the subject, to the need for an examination of the surviving monuments of the Industrial Revolution, not so much in the expectation of obtaining new evidence about their history or construction but in order to understand more fully the extent of their creators' achievement. Few would deny the validity of this approach. It is easy to talk about the two centuries of railway history in Britain before the Stockton and Darlington Railway; to examine the Causey Arch brings a wealth of new meaning to the proposition. The Menai suspension bridge can be just one item in a catalogue of Thomas Telford's achievements; to see the bridge and walk over it remains to this day an awe-inspiring experience. James Watt's parallel motion can be presented as a rather dull innovation in engineering or mechanics; to watch the motion at close quarters on a working beam-engine reveals that it was a thing of beauty as well as usefulness.

To urge historians of the Industrial Revolution to be aware of major monuments was perhaps necessary in 1955, but it was in fact nothing more revolutionary than to urge students of the Renaissance to study

Fig. 13 The world's first multi-storied iron-framed building. Built in 1796–97 to the design of Charles Bage, as the flax mill of Messrs Marshall, Benyon and Bage. 177 feet long and nearly 40 feet wide, it is now dwarfed by many late nineteenth-century mills. Although its appearance is much altered by the filling in of windows, it remains one of Britain's most important industrial monuments.

the Pieta or the Virgin of the Rocks or to suggest that military historians might gain something from visits to Balaclava or Waterloo. Moreover, taken on its own, this sort of approach is not without its dangers. Frequently an innovation which was remarkable in its time can be dwarfed by subsequent developments, so that archaeological study alone can effectively detract from our appreciation of the builder's achievement. One example of this process of devaluation by time is Robert Stephenson's High Level Bridge over the Tyne, from which two other bridges at the same level are now visible. These make it difficult simply from looking at the bridge to appreciate what a revolutionary innovation it was in the 1840s to carry a railway on iron arches from cliff top to cliff top over the Tyne from Durham to Northumberland and, more remarkable still, to suspend a roadway beneath its arches. Similarly in the age of the skyscraper it is difficult to be impressed at first sight with early factory buildings, even with one as imposing as the Marshall, Benyon and Bage flax mill (Fig. 13) in Shrewsbury, unless one is fully aware of the historical context.

Simply looking at the major monuments of the Industrial Revolution is therefore to be commended, but it should not be expected to add very much to our knowledge, even if it does increase our appreciation of the past. One of the misleading ideas about industrial archaeology which has derived from the aesthetic approach is that the subject consists of nothing more than looking, and often of looking not only at major monuments but at various cast-iron ephemera. The study of Victorian pillar boxes or of ornamental manhole covers may be an amusing historical diversion, it may add a little to some very minor branches of historical knowledge, but it is not going to change our understanding of industrial history significantly.

It is from this sort of approach that industrial archaeology has gained the somewhat low position in the league table of academic respectability which it currently occupies. Recognition of the subject in universities has been confined largely to extra-mural departments, and many economic historians regard it with some apprehension. Certainly it is an appealing and popular term. Organisers of adult education programmes will be uncomfortably aware that a course on economic history of doubtful popularity can be made into a considerable crowd-puller if it is called a series on industrial archaeology, whether the approach is strictly archaeological or not. The recent television series 'Industrial Grand Tour', grudgingly granted an inadequate ten-minute slot on Thursday evenings in mid-summer, proved to have considerably higher viewing figures than better-placed programmes on classical archaeology. In a wider sphere, the success of so many railway and (more recently) canal preservation schemes, although some at least can hardly be called archaeological, similarly bears witness to popular interest in an approach to industrial history through working relics, and the embryo industrial open-air museums show every indication of achieving the same levels of popularity.

Much of what has been written about industrial archaeology has perhaps over-emphasised what *can* or *ought* to be done. There have been too many pundits ready to advise others on what lines of research they should follow, and too few works of real excellence completed. Fortunately there are now some hopeful signs of change, and it is becoming possible to show something of the benefits which can come through an archaeological approach to industrial history.

Most writers about industrial archaeology have been agreed that one of its strengths is that it is a re-integrating, multi-disciplinary study. It encompasses a wide range of different techniques; those of the architectural historian, of the historian of technology, of the economic historian working with documents, of the excavating archaeologist, of the metallurgist, of the chemist and of the surveyor. One disadvantage of this situation is that there are no agreed methods of presenting results. The classical or medieval archaeologist has an accepted formula in which he will publish the results of his excavations. No such agreement seems possible in presenting findings about such diverse subjects as factory buildings, river improvements or the excavation of bloomeries. What unifies industrial archaeology, and what characterises much of the best work in the subject, is a disciplined way of looking rather than a specific mode of presentation.

Many of the techniques of industrial archaeology are not new. The architectural historian has perfectly adequate means of presenting evidence about buildings which evolved long before 1955. The historian of technology has known for many decades how to describe a particular type of spinning jenny or valve gear. Industrial archaeology should be a form of what Christopher Taylor has described as 'total history' applied in an industrial context. It is the study, not just of the mechanics of particular bits of apparatus, not just leets, dams and millpools, not just of the roof structures of cotton mills between 1800 and 1820, but of all of the factors which make up the industrial context: buildings, machinery, power sources, workers' and masters' accommodation, and transport systems. Its relationship to other disciplines can perhaps be illustrated with an analogy from earlier periods of archaeology. The historian of technology of earlier decades tended to study the steam engine or the power loom rather as the classical archaeologist of old studied Roman coins, by taking them out of their context. The industrial archaeologist attempts to study the whole industrial context in an integrated way, just as the Roman or medieval archaeologist now works by total stripping. And similarly the industrial archaeologist will need the specialist, the historian of technology, the architect or the chemist, just as the conventional or traditional archaeologist needs the numismatist to deal with his stratified coins.

Industrial archaeology and the landscape

Elsewhere in this volume Christopher Taylor discusses the need for a broadly based approach to landscape history, and the industrial archaeologist certainly needs to be disciplined in this sense so that he does not allow himself to interpret everything he sees in industrial terms. The subject has suffered considerably from the type of enthusiast who may see Ely cathedral as a large building important only for the very exciting Victorian cast-iron heating stoves it contains. At the same time the landscape historian needs to be fully aware of the nature and remains of past industries. The concentration of so much industrial activity in this country on the coalfield regions in the eighteenth and nineteenth centuries has understandably dulled our general appreciation of how much industry there was in every part of the country before 1750. A bank of earth may be glacial morain, a long barrow or a medieval defensive work; it may equally well be a mill dam or a primitive railway embankment. The landscape historian needs to be as fully aware of the latter as of the former. A sheet of water may be a medieval fishpond, a Capability Brown lake or a seventeenth-century furnace pool. It could well have been all three at different periods.[3] And this knowledge should extend to some understanding of industrial techniques. Quite apart from monuments, industrial waste products often form important elements of the landscape. Knowing what is a pit heap and what is a round barrow, what is forge slag and what is volcanic rock, may be necessary for a complete explanation of the landscape seen around us.

Buildings and documents

While archaeological studies can thus make unique and important contributions to our understanding of industrial history, it is absurd to suggest that they can ever be totally divorced from documentary work, although the proportions of documentary and archaeological investigation which can be devoted to a given problem will of course be infinitely variable. The simplest form of archaeological study is the examination and appreciation of a surviving monument, the benefits and dangers of which have been discussed above. Beyond that stage comes the critical study of industrial sites in areas where there may be few surviving monuments but where documentary evidence is plentiful. This is an area of study where documentary and archaeological approaches may come fruitfully into conflict. The historian's delvings into account books and correspondence may well upset the model which the geographer prepares as a result of his fieldwork, although the historian's findings may become more meaningful by expression in terms of the model.

A good example of this sort of conflict can be found in the well-known Coalbrookdale ironworks. This is frequently quoted as a model ironworking site. It stands alongside a reliable stream which powered its waterwheels, near to the confluence with a major commercial river navigation. To the north are hills where coal and iron ore are abundant, while one side of the valley is a massive limestone outcrop (Fig. 14). Examination of the site leads inevitably to a discussion of flow-lines, of the raw materials passing downhill to the furnaces, of pig iron passing from the furnaces to the forges lower in the valley, and the wrought iron from the forges to the river barges. Certainly in some periods the model worked in that fashion, but analysis of the company accounts shows that for long periods limestone came not from Lincoln Hill in

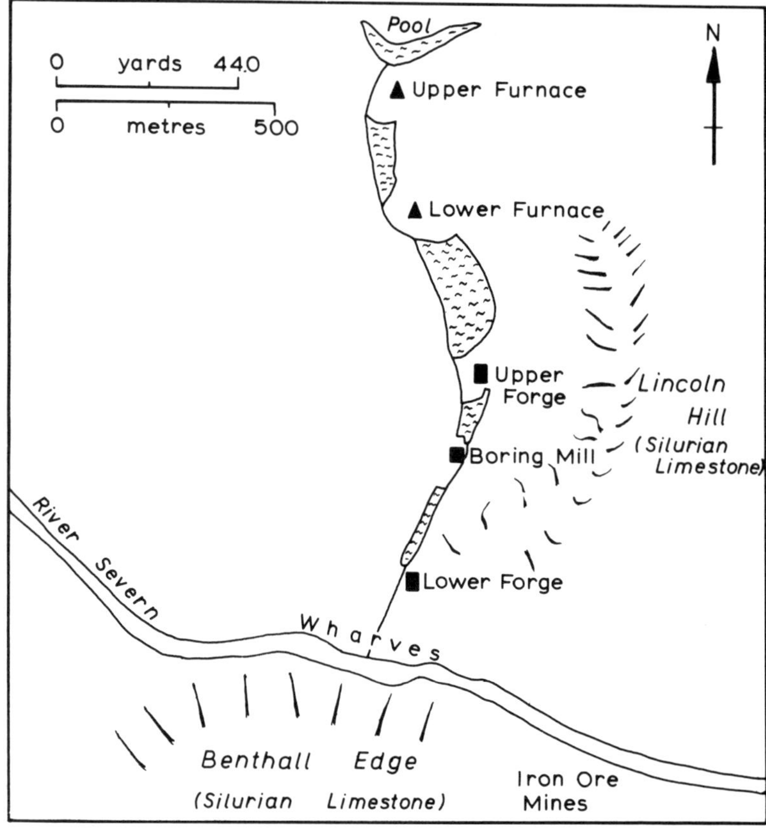

Fig. 14 Lincoln Hill and Boring Mill

Coalbrookdale but from Benthall Edge south of the Severn and from the Much Wenlock area four miles away. Appreciable quantities of iron ore came not from the hills to the north but from south of the Severn, and had to be ferried expensively across the river and clumsily humped uphill on packhorses to the furnaces. The pig iron from these furnaces for metallurgical reasons was not suitable for use at the forges, which were in fact supplied from ironworks all over the West Midlands and even from the American colonies. This is a case where archaeological and documentary interpretations of a site may conflict but where they do not contradict. The historian does not prove the fieldworker wrong, he provides facts which by their exceptional nature illuminate the fieldworker's generalisation. The historian's explanation is more telling when related in terms of the fieldworker's model.

Similar conflicts of evidence can arise over workers' housing. Rows of terraced cottages erected near to a factory can easily be explained as accommodation built by an entrepreneur for his work-people. Nevertheless this too is an area where a dialogue between documents and fieldwork is essential and illuminating. One interesting case is the Cherwell area of Banbury, a district of mean streets, now largely demolished, which numerous books on the town have credited to Bernhard Samuelson who in 1849 took over and substantially enlarged an ironfoundry in the vicinity. On the ground this seems a thoroughly logical explanation. The houses were near to the foundry, and they did have every characteristic which one might expect of workers' cottages of the mid-nineteenth century. Yet the documents show a different picture. The streets were laid out and many houses built and occupied three or four years before Samuelson bought the foundry, and the 1851 census shows that only a very small proportion of the inhabitants were foundry workers. Again, the historian explaining the history of the works can only benefit from examining the site, just as the fieldworker explaining the site can only gain from knowing something of the documents. By introducing new variables and new features to be explained, even the most elementary forms of archaeological investigation can expand our understanding of industrial history.

One healthy effect of the debate about industrial archaeology has been that fewer economic historians would now venture to write about subjects and sites of which they have not examined the physical remains, even if their principal sources are documentary ones. There are some exceptions. One recent survey of turnpike roads, admirably stimulating in many respects, showed no signs that the author had any clear concept of what a turnpike road actually looked like. But industrial archaeology is more than an obligatory stimulant to the economic historian who works from documents; it can in some cases make substantial contributions of its own to our historical understanding. It remains to examine some of the ways in which this has been done.

The contribution of industrial archaeology

One excellent example comes at a very low level of technology, the primitive railway or waggonway. Dr Michael Lewis has shown that there evolved in Great Britain in the seventeenth and eighteenth centuries two distinct types of railway, the Tyneside and Shropshire systems, and that many of the railways built according to the latter principles adopted John Curr's angled cast-iron plate rail in the closing years of the eighteenth century.[4] Many of Dr Lewis's arguments of necessity are based on documentary sources. It is just not possible to see an eighteenth-century wooden railway in operational condition. But there are many aspects of early railways which can only be studied through archaeological methods. In the absence of detailed accounts, it is often impossible to gain from documents any idea of the scale of investment involved in the construction of primitive railways. The tracing of routes and the noting of the dimensions of embankments, cuttings and bridges at least give some indication of this, even if the information they reveal is not precisely quantifiable. Again, archaeological evidence alone reveals substantial regional differences in the operation of primitive railways: that in most parts of Britain plateways consisted of 'stone blocks and iron rails', but that in the ironmaking district of Shropshire cast-iron sleepers were used almost universally instead of stone blocks. Documents reveal only that there was in the nineteenth century a dense network of primitive railways in east Shropshire serving the coal mines and ironworks. Archaeological evidence shows that these railways were bewilderingly varied, that each of the major iron-making concerns had its own pattern if not several patterns of track, that there were at least six different gauges employed, that rail lengths varied from four to fifteen feet, that some lines were haphazardly laid on the surface of the ground, while others were expensively engineered with longitudinal wooden sleepers beneath the rails and carefully laid brick horse-paths between them. Such a confusion of practices must certainly have tended to ossify the existing lines of communication. To switch supplies from one works to another might well have involved rebuilding a railway. Such an inflexible system of transport does not wholly explain the decline of the Shropshire iron industry in the late nineteenth century, but it does go some way towards explaining why the collapse of that industry after 1870 was so precipitate. The plateway is a humble but important aspect of industrial technology of which we can find only limited information in documentary sources. Archaeological investigation has revealed facts and posed questions which could never have been revealed in any other way.

The study of the remains of turnpike roads can similarly help to answer important historical problems. Many roads have of course been altered beyond recognition in the age of the motor car, but some remain sufficiently unaltered to be able to provide answers to questions about the scale of investment in roads in the eighteenth century and the intentions of particular groups of turnpike trustees. Where stretches of turnpike road were by-passed before modern times, or where it is known that the essential structures of modern roads have been unaltered since turnpike days, it is possible to gather much useful information by the surveying of cuttings and embankments, and in the case of by-passed roads by the measuring of carriageway widths. The study of mileposts can, like that of pillar boxes or manhole covers, be a wholly fruitless antiquarian activity, and alas it now seems that the collection of actual mileposts is becoming as popular as the looting of railway relics. Nevertheless mileposts can answer many questions. The destinations quoted on them may reveal something of the intentions and aspirations of the turnpike trustees, and at an early stage of research they may give clues as to which turnpike trust a particular section of road belonged to, something which cannot always be readily discovered from the most easily available documentary sources. On the road from Ironbridge to Bridgnorth the distances to Shrewsbury marked on the cast-iron mileposts show something of the efforts that were made by a number of authorities to develop the route from Shrewsbury to the south by way of Ironbridge at the expense of the older turnpike road by way of Much Wenlock. Turnpike roads have often been quoted as legitimate objects of archaelogical study. It is essential to realise that mileposts, embankments and toll-houses can be used to explain historical problems. They are not just ornaments to be admired.

The study of river navigations in the West Midlands has provided some interesting examples of the value of archaeological evidence. On the Dick Brook in Worcestershire the survival of two undoubted flash locks is one of the best indications of how the most insignificant streams could be made navigable, although the problems associated with the dating of the locks and the various other masonry remains along the brook, await resolution. On a larger tributary of the Severn, a lock probably of the early eighteenth century at the confluence with the River Tern has always been visible, but it had passed unnoticed by historians of the river trade until a fieldworker with training in Roman archaeology noticed it and brought it to general attention. It has since been excavated and surveyed, and provides convincing evidence that at least a short stretch of the River Tern was once navigable. Another problem relating to the Severn shows once more the need to study landscape in the widest possible context. Until recently no explanation has ever been offered of the small islands to be found every few miles along the Severn. It has generally been assumed that they were of natural origin. Recent studies[5] at the Preston Montford Field Studies Centre, originally geomorphologically based, suggest that they are the result of the cutting of gutters for barges to avoid fish weirs. The surviving islands correlate very closely to a list of fish weirs compiled in 1575. The navigations on unimproved rivers like the Severn and most of its tributaries are singularly ill-documented and must continue to present many problems to the historian. Archaeological evidence in this sort of situation can considerably expand our knowledge.

One of the aspects of the Industrial Revolution on which the most conclusive evidence has been gathered in the last twenty-five years has been on the early iron-framed factory buildings. Before the Second World War no one could have imagined that the world's first cast-iron framed textile mill still survived, but the researches of Turpin Bannister and of Skempton and Johnson have not only revealed that it does exist, but have related it to other structures marking the transition from traditional construction to iron-framing. Bannister, Skempton and Johnson[6] employed no special techniques of industrial archaeology, merely those to which architectural historians have grown accustomed. Yet their work is based very largely on the study of the physical remains of the buildings and could not have been nearly so conclusive if based on documentary sources alone.

Area surveys based on fieldwork have illuminated a number of historical problems which could not be answered through documentary studies. In Northumberland surveys of power sources on farms in the era of high farming have shown that there was a real choice between horse, water and steam power. Records of particular farms illuminate the situation, but the choices made on every farm can only be discovered through fieldwork. Similarly surveys of mills in several parts of the country have revealed sites whose existence is not indicated in documentary sources, which can only be discovered by a careful examination of the entire length of the banks of every stream.

One of the most spectacular achievements of industrial archaeologists has been the development of techniques of analysing slags and other waste industrial products, principally the work of the late Reg Morton of Wolverhampton Polytechnic and other members of the Historical Metallurgy Research Group. As a result of laboratory analysis it is now possible to show what raw materials were used in particular processes and what temperatures were reached, and to make deductions about the qualities of the finished products. There remain many problems about the application of these techniques. Analysis of the contents of an excavated furnace reveals only what processes were used in the last days of its operation, which may not have been typical of a working life of two centuries. Analysis of slags taken at random from a tip reveals only what happened on one occasion. It is only with the evolution of better sampling methods and close relationship to documentary investigation that this type of research will fulfil its considerable potential.

Like many of the other approaches to history described in this volume, industrial archaeology remains in its infancy. The corpus of published works of real excellence remains disturbingly small. It is to be hoped that the spate of recently published general introductions to the subjects will not for too long prolong the debate about what industrial archaeology is or what it should be. The subject needs less pundits and more practitioners. Perhaps the most encouraging signs in recent years have been the increasing attention paid to physical remains in works which are in the main based on documentary sources, and the broadening support for the preservation of industrial monuments. We must await with interest those works yet to be written on water mills, early factory buildings, agricultural power sources, river navigations, primitive railways and turnpike roads where the major approach is through fieldwork.

Notes

1 For example Angus Buchanan, *Industrial Archaeology in Britain* (1972); Arthur Raistrick, *Industrial Archaeology* (1972); Kenneth Hudson, *A Guide to the Industrial Archaeology of Europe* (1971); and review of above by R. L. Hills in *West Midlands Studies*, Vol. 5 (Summer 1972); Michael Rix, *Industrial Archaeology* (Historical Association, 1967).

2 Michael Rix, *Amateur Historian* III (1955) pp. 225–29.

3 R. A. Chaplin, 'Discovering lost ironworks', *Local Historian* IX (1970) pp. 82–88.

4 M. J. T. Lewis, *Early Wooden Railways* (1970).

5 David Pannett, 'Fish weirs of the River Severn', *Shropshire Newsletter* No. 41 (Sept. 1971).

6 T. C. Bannister, 'The first iron-frame building', *Architectural Review*, CVII (1950); A. W. Skempton and H. R. Johnson, 'The first iron frames', *ibid.*, CXXXI (1962).